NAGALAND

NAGALAND

VERRIER ELWIN

GYAN

Published by

Gyan Publishing House
5, Ansari Road
Daryaganj, New Delhi-110002
Phone: 011-47034999, 9811692060
E-mail: books@gyanbooks.com

Distribution Network
gyanbooks.com
India, USA, Canada, UK, Australia

ISBN: 978-93-6280-383-2 (PB)
First Published, 1961

2nd Impression 2024

Printed at: Gyan Press, Delhi.

NAGALAND
Author: VERRIER ELWIN

NAGALAND

ALSO BY VERRIER ELWIN

The Baiga (Murray, 1939)
The Agaria (O.U.P., 1942)
Maria Murder and Suicide (O.U.P., 1943, second edition, 1950)
Folk-Tales of Mahakoshal (O.U.P., 1944)
Folk-Songs of Chhattisgarh (O.U.P., 1946)
The Muria and their Ghotul (O.U.P., 1947). French edition, *Maisons des Jeunes chez les Muria* (Gallimard, 1959)
Myths of Middle India (O.U.P., 1949)
Bondo Highlander (O.U.P., 1950)
The Tribal Art of Middle India (O.U.P., 1951)
Tribal Myths of Orissa (O.U.P., 1954)
The Religion of an Indian Tribe (O.U.P., 1955)
A Philosophy for NEFA (NEFA Administration, Shillong, 1957, second edition, 1959, reprinted 1960)
Myths of the North-East Frontier of India (NEFA, 1958)
India's North-East Frontier in the Nineteenth Century (O.U.P., 1959)
The Art of the North-East Frontier of India (NEFA, 1959)
The Hill People of North-East India (O.U.P., 1960)

NAGALAND

VERRIER ELWIN

SHILLONG
1961

PUBLISHED BY P. DUTTA FOR THE RESEARCH DEPARTMENT,
ADVISER'S SECRETARIAT, SHILLONG

First edition: 5,000 copies

Price Rs. 15.00

PRINTED BY S. N. GUHA RAY AT SREE SARASWATY PRESS LTD.,
32 ACHARYA PROFULLA CHANDRA ROAD, CALCUTTA-9

TO

MY BELOVED

LILA

'The problem of the tribal areas is to make the people feel that they have perfect freedom to live their own lives and to develop according to their wishes and genius. India to them should signify not only a protecting force but a liberating one. Any conception that India is ruling them and that they are the ruled, or that customs and habits with which they are unfamiliar are going to be imposed upon them, will alienate them.'

—JAWAHARLAL NEHRU

CONTENTS

LIST OF ILLUSTRATIONS

HALF-TONES

LINE-DRAWINGS

PHOTO: P. PAL

SCENERY BELOW MERANGKONG IN *the Ao Naga area*

Nagaland over a century ago. Reproduced from John Butler's *Travels and Adventures in the Province of Assam* (London, 1855)

I

A FINE PEOPLE

On the 1st of August 1960, Mr Jawaharlal Nehru told India's Lok Sabha (House of Commons) that his Government had decided to create a new, sixteenth State within the Indian Union to be known as Nagaland. Although this was hardly noticed by the world at large, it was the most momentous and exciting occasion in the extraordinary history of an extraordinary people. For years the Nagas had been clamouring and struggling for some sort of autonomy. Had they realised it, the essentials of this had been for years within their grasp. For, as the Prime Minister said in his speech at the time, 'Our policy has always been to give the fullest autonomy and opportunity of self-development to the Naga people, without interfering in any way in their internal affairs or way of life.'

'India', he said again, 'achieved her independence thirteen years ago and the Nagas are as independent as other Indian citizens. We have not the slightest desire to interfere in the tribal customs and usage of the Nagas or in their distinctive way of life' and in the new State they should be able to find 'the fullest opportunity for self-expression'.

Who are these Nagas, for whom India has offered so much sympathy, given such special privileges and felt such great concern ? They are an Indo-Mongoloid folk living in the north-eastern hills of India, divided into over a dozen major tribes, speaking more than a dozen languages and dialects, formerly notorious for head-hunting, which is almost the only thing most people know about them, but today awake and stirring, anxious to progress. They are a fine people, of whom their country is proud, strong and self-reliant, with the free and independent outlook characteristic of highlanders everywhere, good to look at, with an unerring instinct for colour and design, friendly and cheerful with a keen sense of humour, gifted with splendid dances and a love of song.

The Kiratas

The great authority of Dr S. K. Chatterji, supported by other scholars, considers that the classical word 'Kirata' is the equivalent of what today we call 'Indo-Mongoloid', a word which itself is useful as defining both the Indian connection of the people to whom it applies and their place within the cultural milieu in which they have established themselves, as well as their original racial affinities, and he includes among them 'all those Sino-Tibetan-speaking tribes, Mongoloids of various types in race, who entered into or touched the fringe of the cultural entity that is India—the Himalayan tribes (the Nepal tribes and the North-Assam tribes), the Bodos and the Nagas, the Kuki-Chins, the Ahoms, the Indian Tibetans, the Khasis, and the earlier tribes (of unknown affiliation within the Tibeto-Burman branch of the Sino-Tibetan family) who have now become absorbed in the populations of the plains of northern and north-eastern India.'

There are four or five million Indo-Mongoloids, including the Nagas, and some of them have been in India for a very long time, their presence being first noted in the tenth century before Christ, at the time of the compilation of the Vedas. From this time onwards the word 'Kirata' was used for the non-Aryan tribes living in the mountains, particularly in the Himalayas and in the north-eastern areas of India, who were clearly distinguished from the tribes of Austric origin, the Sabaras, Pulindas, Nishadas and Bhillas, who were settled elsewhere.

The ancient Sanskrit literature describes them as hillmen living mostly on game, fruit and roots, dressing in skins, warlike and wielding formidable weapons. They were a good-looking folk and there is constant stress on their 'gold-like' colour in contrast to the dark skin of the other pre-Aryan people of the plains. These early Kiratas were rich with the natural wealth of minerals and forest produce of their mountains and were adepts in the art of weaving cloth, as the Nagas still are; in ancient as well as modern times the fabrics they made have been greatly in demand in the plains. An exhibition of Naga art held in Delhi at the beginning of 1960 came as a revelation to many who had no idea of their creative achievements.

Some Kiratas became Hindus, some Buddhists, recently a few have become Christians. Their importance in Hindu tradition is indicated by the fact that Siva Mahadeva, the great God, is described, as early as the *Mahabharata*, as taking the form of a Kirata, with Uma beside him as a Kirata woman, and going together to meet Arjuna. It is possible that Buddha himself was an Indo-Mongoloid or Kirata and through him India has a spiritual link with the whole Buddhist Mongoloid world.

In Assam other famous Indo-Mongoloid tribes are first the Bodos, linguistically connected with the Nagas, who spread all over the Brahmaputra Valley and occupied the Garo Hills, ultimately leaving their mark throughout the whole of Assam. Later Indo-Mongoloid immigrants were the Asams or Ahoms who established themselves in the east of the Brahmaputra Valley at the beginning of the thirteenth century and gave their name to Assam. By the middle of the sixteenth century they had conquered the powerful Bodo kingdom of the Kacharis and ruled over Assam until the British annexed the Province in 1824.

We need not detain ourselves with an account of the other Indo-Mongoloid elements in the general Indian population, except to note that they have always been significant and that the Licchavis, the Newars, the Koches and Kacharis along with others have contributed to the evolution of Indian culture for the last three thousand years and they have had an important place in Indian history, beginning with the battle of Kurukshetra. As a result of their long isolation and lack of cohesion as a single people, the Nagas have hitherto been denied this, but now there will be every opportunity for them to take their share in the Indian renaissance of today.

There has been a tendency to regard the Nagas as a lonely island isolated amidst an alien culture in which the rest of India took little interest. History, however, shows that they form part of an important branch of the great and varied Indian family.

The Naga Countryside

Nagaland, which is now divided into three Districts—Kohima, Mokokchung and Tuensang—with its administrative headquarters at Kohima town, is a long narrow strip of hills running more or less parallel to the south or left bank of the Brahmaputra. If we take Manipur as the southern base, then Nagaland will ascend across the map in a north-easterly direction, with Burma to the east, the Tirap Frontier Division of the North-East Frontier Agency (NEFA) to the north and the broad valley of the Assam plains all along the western foothills. The entire country is covered with ranges of hills, which sometimes break into a wild chaos of spurs and ridges, and sometimes, as round Kohima, descend with gentler slopes. Most villages stand at three to four thousand feet, though some hills rise above them to six thousand and the highest peak in Kohima District is Japvo, at 9,890 feet. The main concentrations of population, very typical of the Nagas, are on the tops of hills and at the higher elevations, and the unhealthy foothills towards the plains are only thinly populated. Rainfall is sufficient but not excessive, averaging 70″ to 100″ in the year, and there are many rivers and streams, but no lakes or tanks.

There is still a great deal of forest left, but much has fallen before the axe of the shifting cultivator and most of the wild game has been lost to the hunter's spear. Wild elephants and buffaloes, tigers and leopards, bears and various kinds of deer remain in only small numbers. Among birds, the Great Indian Hornbill is the most treasured, for use in decoration and magic.

The word 'Naga'

The derivation of the word 'Naga' is obscure. It has been explained as meaning 'hillman', from the Sanskrit *naga*, a mountain. It has been linked to the Kachari *naga*, a young man or warrior, Long ago, Ptolemy thought it meant 'naked'. It has nothing to do with snakes.

The most likely derivation—to my mind—is that which traces 'Naga' from the word *nok* or 'people', which is its meaning in a few Tibeto-Burman languages, as in Garo, Nocte and Ao. It is common throughout India for tribesmen to call themselves by words meaning 'man', an attractive habit which suggests that they look on themselves simply as *people*, free of communal or caste associations.

The name, however, was not in general use among the Nagas until recently. It was given them by the people of the plains and in the last century was used indiscriminately for the Abors and Daflas as well as for the Nagas themselves. Even as late as 1954 I found the people of Tuensang rarely speaking of themselves as Nagas but as Konyaks, Changs, Phoms and so on. In the same way the Mikirs usually speak of themselves as Arlengs, the Garos as Achikrangs (hill people), the Abors as Minyongs or Padams. Gradually, however, as the Nagas became more united they began to use the name for themselves, until today it has become widely popular.

The application of the name is equally confused. Dr J. H. Hutton, our greatest authority on these tribes and one of the truest British friends that they have ever had, says that: 'It is generally assumed in a vague sort of way that those tribes which are spoken of as Nagas have something in common with each other which distinguishes them from the many other tribes found in Assam and entitles them to be regarded as a racial unit in themselves. . . The truth is that, if not impossible, it is exceedingly difficult to propound any test by which a Naga tribe can be distinguished from other Assam or Burma tribes which are not Nagas.'

The Naga Groups

At the same time, there is an atmosphere, a spirit, in a Naga which is unmistakable, and is shared by the following tribes inhabiting Nagaland. Until the Census of next year it is only possible to give a rough estimate of their population, but the following figures are, I believe, reasonably accurate.

Angamis	30,000	Mixed tribes	5,000
Aos	50,000	Phoms	13,000
Chakhesangs	31,000	Rengmas	5,000
Changs	17,000	Sangtams	20,700
Khienmungans	17,000	Semas	48,000
Konyaks	63,000	Yimchungrs	17,500
Lothas	23,500	Zeliangs	5,250

There are also 2,400 Kukis in the hills and a mixed community of 8,600 at Dimapur, a small town in the foothills which gives Nagaland rail communication with Assam, making a total population of a little over 3,57,000.

The tribal groups of Nagaland are forming new affiliations and using names hitherto unknown to anthropology. The Chakhesangs, for example, are a combination of Chakru, Khezha (both southern Angami) and Sangtam groups with two Rengma villages living to the east of Kohima and north of Manipur, who adopted the new name about 1946, and the Zeliangs are similarly a mixed group of Zemis, Liangmais and others. The great Konyak tribe consists of two rather sharply distinguished divisions, one ruled by powerful and autocratic chiefs, the other more democratic, which now calls itself Shamnyuyungmang.

Naga Life and Culture

It is very difficult to give a general account of the many tribes covered by the word Naga, for there are both differences and similarities among them just as there are many aspects of their life and culture which can be paralleled by tribes in other parts of India. For example, the Bondos of Orissa resemble in a quite remarkable way the Konyaks of Tuensang.

In physique and appearance the different Naga groups vary considerably, the Angamis, for example, being tall with regular features and the Semas shorter with more strongly pronounced Mongolian features. In colour too there are differences. Most are a beautiful light brown—the typical Kirata 'gold', but differing in shade from tribe to tribe and a light colour is generally admired, though it has been recorded that some Nagas, years ago, expressed their dislike of the 'English' colour, regarding it as unripe or 'undercooked'. There is wavy hair and straight hair and even the Negrito frizzly hair.

Some of the Nagas make great wooden drums or xylophones, splendid instruments which can send their message for several miles. Other groups, however, especially in the south, do not make them at all. Some of the tribes use a reaping-hook for harvesting, but the Semas traditionally only use their hands. The Angamis have excellent terraces and in this they are followed by a few other tribes who have come under their influence, while others do not practise terracing at all, though this type of cultivation has been, to some extent, introduced by Government. Even in methods of sowing there are distinctions. The Angamis, Lhotas, Rengmas and Semas are very careful with their grain, making little holes in the ground and dropping in the seed. The Aos, Changs and Konyaks, however, scatter the seed broadcast. Monoliths used to be set up by the tribes, such as the Angamis, practising terrace cultivation (it is interesting to note that the Saoras of Orissa, who make even better terraces than the Angamis, also put up megalithic monuments for their dead) and by the Lhotas and Rengmas. To the north and east, however, the tribes rarely do this until we reach the Konyaks who erect monoliths for a number of purposes. In traditional funerary practice the Nagas vary greatly, some burning or burying their dead; others, such as the Konyaks, exposing corpses on platforms; while the Khienmungans used to have a practice of desiccation.

Naga society presents a varied pattern of near-dictatorship and extreme democracy. There is a system of hereditary chieftainship among the Semas and Changs. The Konyaks have very powerful Chiefs or Angs who are regarded as sacred and whose word is law:

before the greatest of them no commoner may stand upright. The Aos, however, have bodies of elders who represent the main family groups in the village and the Angamis, Lhotas, Rengmas and others are so democratic that Hutton remarks that in the case of the Angamis it is difficult to comprehend how, in view of their peculiar independence of character, their villages held together at all before the coming of the British Government.

The Naga Villages and Homes

As long ago as 1873 Captain Butler spoke of the Angamis as occupying 'a most charming country, enjoying a beautiful climate and most fertile soil, well cultivated, drained, and manured, the hill-sides being covered with a succession of terraces of rich rice, with numerous villages in every direction, some of them so large that they might justly be called towns.' The size of the villages and their dignity is very striking even in the wilder Tuensang border ranges; they are built on the most commanding points along the ridges of the hills and were formerly stockaded by stone walls, palisades, dykes or fences of thorns, and some had village gates, great wooden doors decorated with painted carvings in bas-relief, which were approached by narrow winding paths sunk in the ground. The Aos and Lhotas arrange their houses in regular streets, often along the top of a ridge; other tribes build as they please; but all divide their villages into *khels* or quarters, each with its own headmen and administration.

Eastern Rengma (after Mills)

The houses themselves are usually fairly large, sometimes very large, and reflect the importance of the owner. Some have high gables projecting in front; others are crowned by crossed wooden horns; the trophies of the chase, and equally the relics of great feasts, are proudly displayed in the front porch. Many houses are built high above the ground on stilts and there is always a sitting-platform at the back.

Prominent in many villages is the Morung or dormitory for the young unmarried men—some tribes also have small houses for the unmarried girls. The Morungs are guard-houses, recreation clubs, centres of education, art and discipline and have an important ceremonial purpose. Many house the great wooden drums which are beaten to summon for war or to announce a festival. Formerly skulls and other trophies of war were hung in the Morungs and the pillars are still carved with striking representations of tigers, hornbills, human figures, monkeys, lizards and elephants.

The staple food of the Nagas is rice supplemented by meat and, except occasionally for individual or clan taboos, they cast their net widely, though they prefer beef and pork. They are now drinking tea and even taking to milk, on which until recently they had a taboo. But their favourite drink is rice-beer, which may be described as a nourishing and palatable soup with a kick in it. For while its alcoholic content is small, it contains most of the essential nutrients and is an important source of Naga energy and strength.

It is impossible to describe Naga dress here, for it varies from tribe to tribe and is changing all the time. We will be content to note that the Nagas are very protocol-minded about dress, and in the old days the finest cloth could be worn only by the head-hunter or the donor of Feasts of Merit. I have given here a number of drawings, based on photographs in the older books, which illustrate various types of traditional attire. It would be hard to beat a Naga in his ceremonial finery, and he makes full use of his natural skill and taste in the use of cowries, feathers, goat's-hair dyed red, shells, bone and ivory. Naga textiles, of great variety, are woven by the women on small loin-looms of an Indonesian pattern.

In the past the Nagas made almost everything for themselves, and some tribes developed a singular competence in the creation of both useful and artistic objects. Their iron work is still expert, and they have a little pottery. They have extraordinary dexterity in the use of bamboo, and with wood some of the tribes, especially perhaps the Konyaks, can produce strong and graceful carvings. The universal implement is the dao, a bill or hatchet, which is used in cultivation, as an effective weapon of war, and as a general tool of all work. Other

A Naga morung (after Shakespear)

weapons are spears and guns—the Konyak forges have turned out simple muzzle-loaders for generations.

The basic interest of every Naga is in his family, the clan, the *khel*, the village. This is what he regards as his culture which must not be interfered with. He is passionately attached to his land, his system of land-tenure, the arrangements for the government of his village, the organization of cultivation, the administration of tribal justice through the village and tribal courts.

Religion

Naga religion is of a type common throughout tribal India. There is a vaguely imagined supreme creator and arbiter of mankind, and many minor deities, ghosts and spirits of trees, rivers, hills: all nature is alive with unseen forces. There are priests and medicine-men who placate these spirits, banish those who give disease, attract those who help and guard, and who take the lead in the rites and festivals which stimulate the processes of agriculture, bless the marriage bed and protect the craftsman at his work.

Naga ideas of the after-life are confused and vary from tribe to tribe, but there is universal agreement that the soul does not perish at death. Some say it goes onward by a narrow path guarded by a spirit with whom it must struggle; some think it finds its final home below the ground, many believe that it takes the form of various insects, especially butterflies; some say that the good soul goes to a Village of the Dead towards the sunrise, the bad to a less pleasant place towards the sunset.

Feasts of Merit

A central feature of traditional Naga life is the giving of what have come to be known as Feasts of Merit, in which the splendour, colour and extravagance of Naga life is concentrated. These Feasts consist, broadly speaking, of a series of ceremonies, in a rising scale of importance, leading finally to the sacrifice of the mithun—that great creature (the *bos frontalis*) which is the chief domestic animal and used almost as currency, to settle a marriage or pay a fine. The Feasts bring the donor honour both now and after death and he can henceforth wear special clothes and ornaments, and decorate his house in a special way. Only a married man can give one of these Feasts, for his wife must take a conspicuous and honoured place in the proceedings.

The Nagas have never shown much interest in Hinduism, but it is interesting to find some agreement between the ceremonial of these

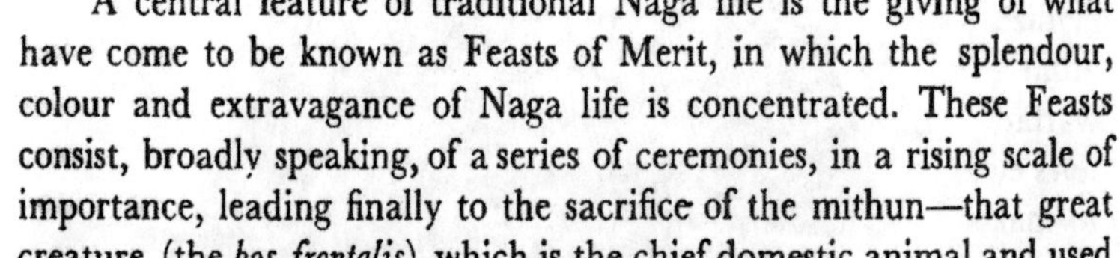

A Naga dao: there are many other types

Feasts and that of the old Vedic religion. In the elaborate sacrifices of the later Vedic age, sheep, goats, cows or oxen and horses were killed. The ceremonies lasted for days and the householder and his wife had to take part. The bull-killing sacrifice and the killing of the mithun in the Naga Feasts are done almost in the Vedic manner, in each case the animal being killed by a sharp stake of wood which pierced its heart, and the important place given to the wife of a man performing these sacrifices is another point of contact.

A mithun

Head-hunting

The practice of head-hunting is found all over the world and has attracted great attention. So-called civilized countries, which can destroy whole populations with a single atom bomb, can hardly afford to look down on a method of ritual warfare which, at the most, involved the loss of a few hundreds of lives every year. The Nagas say that originally they did not know how to make war but one day a bird dropped a berry from a tree, and a lizard and a red ant fought for it. Someone saw the ant cut off the lizard's head and thus men learnt to take heads.

The reasons for head-hunting are complicated and interesting. The practice is probably based on a belief in a soul-matter or vital essence of great power which resides in the human head. By taking a head from another village, therefore, it was believed that a new injection of vital and creative energy would come to the aggressor's village when he brought the head home. This was valuable for human and animal fertility. It stimulated the crops to grow better, especially when the head was that of a woman with long hair. Moreover the Nagas have always been a warlike race and the warrior, especially the young warrior, who had taken a head held a great advantage over his fellows in attracting the most beautiful girl of his village for marriage. Indeed, it is said that a youth who had not taken a head found considerable difficulty in obtaining a wife at all.

Head-hunting was something more than war. It inspired wonderful dances. It stimulated artistic production, for the most elaborate textiles could only be worn by a successful head-hunter or his relations. Small replicas of heads were carved to be worn almost like medals. Wooden pipes, with their bowls fashioned as heads, were made. Strong and vigorous human figures were carved and attached to baskets and the warrior's grave was the most splendid of all.

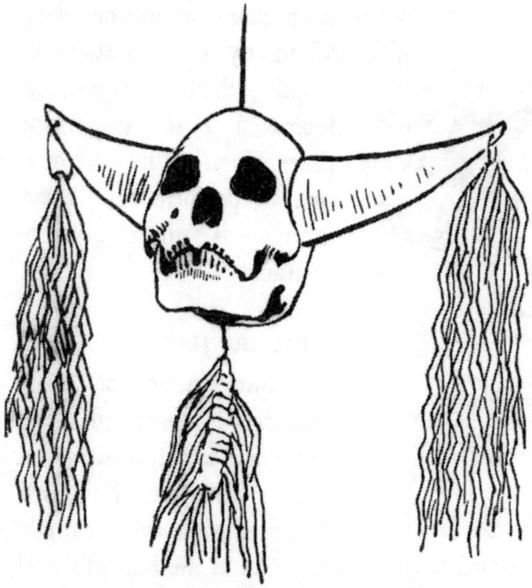

Decorated skull of a head-hunter's victim

Head-hunting virtually ceased soon after the British began to exercise effective control over the Naga Hills area, though it continued in Tuensang until recently. Here also it would probably have died out altogether if it had not been revived as a result of rebel action in the more distant villages. The last recorded case was in 1958.

The Naga Languages

The linguistic topography of Nagaland is remarkable for very complicated and numerous dialectical variations. In some areas the dialect differs from village to village, and in earlier days men and women in the same household sometimes had to use different forms of speech. To this confusion the former division of the people by inter-village feuds undoubtedly contributed. There is, however, a general similarity in the languages and dialects spoken by the Nagas which belong, according to the Linguistic Survey of India, to the Naga group of the Tibeto-Burman family. An American philologist has recently re-classified them, placing the majority of them in what he calls the Burmic division, and a small minority in the Baric division, of the Sino-Tibetan tongues.

The Naga languages, however, possess a number of features which differ from those common to the general Tibeto-Burman family. They are, as Mr Das Shastri, a philologist who has worked in north-eastern India for a number of years, points out, highly tonal; the vowels do not conform to any known definite category and appear to be indistinct; the consonants, specially when they occur at the end of words, are glottalized; aspiration characterizes liquids and nasals; locative variety predominates in the case system and the conjugational pattern presents an extremely rich variety of moods and well classified tenses; negatives are mainly prefixed or suffixed, infixation occurring in a few instances; classificatory terms, both numerical and nominal, are in use,

Within the group lexical resemblances between Angami, Sema, Lhota, Ao and Meitei (Manipuri) have been noted. Morphological resemblances between Ao and Meitei; Angami and Kachari; Ao, Angami and Mikir; and Ao, Angami and Kachari, are very striking.

For a long time past Nagas of different groups have talked to one other either in broken Assamese or in English, and the Nagas themselves observed with some amusement that at a conference at

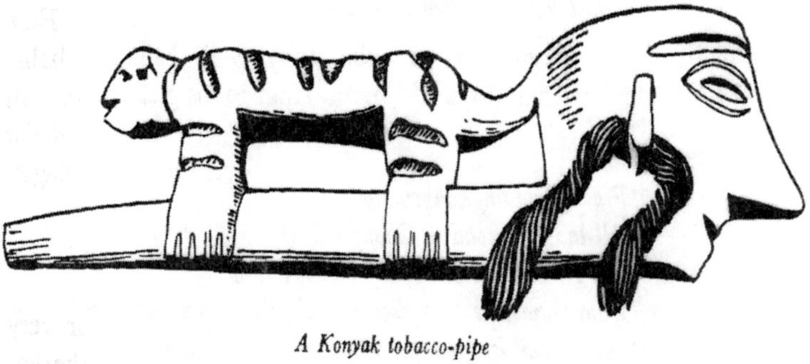

A Konyak tobacco-pipe

which they demanded separation from Assam, many of the speakers made their speeches in the Assamese language. Assamese has been useful to the Nagas for the purposes of trade and to promote unity between the different tribes. Many Nagas now are acquainted with Hindi and English.

Naga Poetry

If we are to judge from the translations from Naga poetry that have been made by various hands from time to time, the people have a high capacity for the purest romantic love and a rich vein of poetic thought which should surely be better known. The Naga passion for beauty and colour, which inspired them to decorate almost everything they used or wore, appears too in their songs which, like all tribal poetry, is not written down but is treasured in the memory and brought out to music. I have seldom heard such beautiful singing as once when at night in a Konyak village high up on the Burmese border, girls sang as they husked rice together in a great mortar. Or again when a group of Chakhesang youths sang a love-song, gradually lowering their voices until it was as if each was whispering into the very ear of his beloved. Girls and boys in fact constantly make love to each other in poetry. 'You are beautiful,' says a Rengma poet, 'as a rhododendron bud and a red berry.' Says an Angami boy:

From youth on let there be no parting
I will wait by the path to watch;
I gaze at that fairest one from afar.
When her hair is long and bound up,
Then will I wait for her at dawn,
I will take her beyond the others.

And in an Ao Naga song (translated by J. P. Mills), a flying squirrel falls in love with a bird and the boy sings to his girl, the bird.

THE SQUIRREL SINGS

From far Lungkungchang
All the long road to Chongliyimti
Have I come to where my beloved sleeps.
I am handsome as a flower, and when I am with my beloved
May dawn linger long below the world's edge.

THE BIRD REPLIES

Countless suitors come to the house where I sleep,
But in this lover only, handsome as a flower,
Do mine eyes behold the ideal of my heart.
Many came to the house where I sleep,
But the joy of my eyes was not among them.
My lover is like the finest bead
On the necks of all the men of all the world.
When my lover comes not to where I sleep,
Ugly and hateful to my eyes is my chamber.

I will also quote a Konyak poem, recorded and translated by C. von Furer-Haimendorf, about two lovers who were in a forbidden relation to each other, and who had to die. The poet does not condemn their love, but idealizes it in the image of the smoke of the separate fires uniting and mingling in death.

Yinglong and Liwang
They loved each other,
Loving, they lay together,
Red as the leaf of the ou-bou tree,
Flamed love and desire.
On the paths to the village,
The two lit fires,
Skywards, upwards curling,
The smoke of the fires united,
And mingled, never to part.

Submerging these cultural specialities (on which I have only had time to touch with extreme brevity) is the great tide of daily life. The ways in which men resemble each other are far more important than those in which they differ. The Nagas, like other people, are concerned first with their daily bread; they are interested in cultivation and trade; they are interested in knowledge, achievement, progress. They are born, they grow up, they love and marry and discover the joys and anxieties of parenthood, the rewards of age, the comfort of religion, they grow old and die. Naturally, you will say, we all do that—and that is just my point: we all do the same things, feel in much the same way, experience pleasure and suffer pain together. In essentials, the Naga is just like everyone else in the world.

A Time of Change

And, like everyone else, the Naga is changing rapidly. This is nothing new: contact with the plains through trade has been continuing for much more than a hundred years: a new religion, an ordered administration, two World Wars, the recent disturbances have had their varied impact, and it does, in fact, say much for the vitality of Naga culture that it has not disappeared altogether.

New accessibility of markets and improved communications have led to the import of many novelties—there are blouses, brassieres, falsies, lipstick for girls: plastic ornaments and celluloid combs usurp the old decorations of shell and bead, bird's-wing and flowers. School-boys have a uniform of shirt and shorts, with gay coloured bush-coats in American style. Brass or aluminium pots take the place of the old bamboo vessels for cooking and drawing water, enamel mugs replace the old bamboo vessels which were sometimes skilfully carved or decorated with poker-work; there are electric torches, petromaxes, chairs and tables, smart walking-shoes, fashionable hats of every kind.

But the real changes go much deeper. The fundamental difference has come in shifting the gear of life from war to peace, the cessation of head-hunting and the gradual disappearance of the Feasts of Merit. This has led to all sorts of unexpected consequences. It is no longer possible to wear some of the finest products of Naga textile art, for these depended on success in war or generosity in feasting. Wood-carving has suffered for the same reason. The architecture of houses has changed, for certain features could only be added by families who had earned the right to do so. The maintenance of the morungs is no longer urgent, now that there is no need to keep a guard always on duty.

Conversion to Christianity has made other changes : the stress on personal salvation has introduced a new individualism in place of the former community spirit. Hymns have taken the place of the old songs; many dances, which celebrated head-hunting raids, cannot now be danced or simply linger on for exhibition to important visitors. Among the newly educated there is, as all over the world in similar circumstances, a turning away from the land, a reluctance to work with one's own hands, a desire for white-collar jobs.

In some ways, however, the last few years have witnessed a revival of Naga culture. Except for a few 'modern' girls, nearly all the women retain much of their hand-woven dress. Even the Christian Nagas are showing a new interest in their traditional dances : they want to build up their own literature in their own languages, to record their old epics and stories; they are developing a sense of history.

They are, in fact, beginning to feel that there is less conflict between yesterday and tomorrow than they had once feared. Their innate sense of beauty, their good taste, their own self-reliance will probably maintain the tradition of weaving and other arts. And the old life on the hillside, in the forest or by the mountain stream, which was a good life, will continue, and the stories and ideas of the country-side will survive, but with new motives and a new direction.

Konyak warrior

II

THE NAGAS IN HISTORY

For hundred of years the Nagas have passed through stormy weather. At the beginning of the thirteenth century the Shan Chief Sukhapa crossed the Patkoi Range dividing India and Burma and subjugated the Nagas and other tribes. It is recorded that his treatment of them cast a heavy cloud on his reputation; he caused some of his Naga prisoners to be killed and their bodies roasted, compelling their relatives to eat their flesh.

The Nagas and the Ahoms

Naga relation with the Ahoms reveals a rather curious blend of hostility and friendliness. The Ahom kings regarded the Nagas as their subjects and took taxes from them in the form of slaves, elephant tusks, spears, hand-woven cloth and cotton. They granted the Naga Chiefs land and retainers just as if they were Assamese nobles. Their estates were managed by Assamese officials called Naga-Kakatis. The son of a Naga Chief was given the important official post of Barphukan. There are persistent legends in the hills about an Ahom king who took refuge with the Nagas and was treated by them with characteristic hospitality.

In the sixteenth and seventeenth centuries, however, there were a number of clashes between the Nagas and their Ahom rulers. About 1530, a body of Nagas defeated an Ahom force and captured several guns. In another clash, in 1692, the Nagas killed twenty-three Assamese subjects. For this King Gadadhar Singh took severe revenge, executing one of the Naga Chiefs and forcing other leaders to visit the capital and reaffirm their allegiance. Shortly afterwards there was another rebellion, but it was subdued and the Nagas, though claiming that it was really the fault of the Abors, are said to have presented Gadadhar Singh with two of their Chiefs' daughters, along with their slaves and attendants. Nagas were recruited into the Ahom forces and were 'quite able to hold their own against well-trained armies'.

Shihabuddin, the Moghal chronicler, who went with Mir Jumla's expedition to Assam in 1662, wrote that although most of the inhabitants of the neighbouring hills, who obviously include the Nagas, paid no tax to the Raja of Assam, 'yet they accept his sovereignty and obey some of his commands'. It has been suggested that one reason for the success of the Ahoms in dealing with the Nagas and other tribes was their freedom from caste prejudice and one of the rare references to the tribes in the *Buranjis* (the old historical records of Assam) relates the great satisfaction of the tribes when Ahom soldiers ate with them in their houses. The Mikirs said, 'These men eat the things we eat; they are therefore men of our fraternity.' It is pleasant to find in the long narrative of conflict such evidence of friendliness and toleration.

The British Occupation of Assam

It is likely that the Nagas bore their share of suffering during the troubled years at the end of the eighteenth century which led to the intervention of the British Government and the Anglo-Burmese war which reached its conclusion in 1824. The historian Mackenzie describes how the British, who first came into regular contact with the Nagas about 1832, found 'the Assam Valley surrounded north, east, and south by numerous savage and warlike tribes whom the decaying authority of the Assam dynasty had failed of late years to control, and whom the disturbed condition of the Province had incited to encroachment. Many of them advanced claims to rights more or less definite over lands lying in the plains; others claimed tributary payments from the villages below their hills, or the services of Paiks said to have been assigned them by the Assam authorities. It mattered, of course, little to us whether these claims had their basis in primaeval rights from which the Shan invaders had partially ousted the hillmen, or whether they were merely the definite expression of a barbarian cupidity. Certain it was that such claims existed, and that they had been, to some extent and in some places, formally recognised by our predecessors. The engagements under which the Native Governments lay were transferred to the British who tried to reconcile them with the "requirements of enlightened policy".'

The British occupation of Assam did not, however, bring the troubles of the Nagas to an end. The Singphos, at that time a warlike and aggressive tribe, seem to have sought by conquest of the Nagas to supply the deficiency of slave labour which was a consequence of Assam's annexation. In 1837 a party of British officers returning from Burma across the Patkoi met a war party of Singphos fresh from the sack of Naga villages and dragging along gangs of prisoners. Since already 'all upon this frontier that was not Burmese was regarded as actual British territory', these officers had no scruples about interfering to deliver the Naga captives.

The Nagas and Manipur

A few years earlier, in the cold season of 1832-33, Raja Gumbhir Singh of Manipur, who had the ambition of achieving the permanent conquest of the Naga Hills, marched through Naga territory from Imphal to Assam. The British Government was not entirely happy about this, but it came to be supposed 'in a general way that Manipur exercised some sort of authority' over the southern portion of the Naga Hills. In 1835, Naga exactions and raids on the hill villages of North Cachar inspired Government to place the responsibility of controlling them on a powerful local Chief, Tularam, and the Manipur State. The Commissioner of Assam did not like this, for Manipur troops got no pay, had to live on the plunder of the villages they occupied, and the ferocity of their raids fully equalled those of the Nagas. The Government, says Mackenzie, was inclined to regard the Manipuris as the *de facto* masters of the hills, and it persisted in calling upon Manipur to occupy the country of the Angamis, sending a detachment of sepoys under a European officer to check any needless outrages. Local officials and the Court of Directors opposed this policy and after two or three years it was reversed, and a British civilian was sent into the Angami Hills, where he received a friendly reception from a number of villages.

Among the villages which Gumbhir Singh reduced to submission was Kohima itself and a stone was set up and his footprints were sculptured on it in token of conquest. Sir James Johnstone declares that 'the Nagas greatly respected this stone and cleaned it from time to time. They opened a large trade with Manipur, and whenever a Manipuri visited a Naga village he was treated as an honoured guest.'

Naga Raids

For the next hundred years the British Government could not make up its mind about the north-eastern tribal areas. They were in the position of a man who has a large garden which he does not quite know what to do with. Its boundaries and extent are clear but to cultivate it properly he needs a small army of gardeners, which he can ill afford. So he clears part of it, removes the weeds and raises flowers, but leaves the rest in its wild yet attractive state, waiting for a day when he has greater leisure and more money; sometimes he has a spurt of energy and clears a little more; he often walks round his possessions; but on the whole he leaves the uncultivated part alone, even though his friends criticise him for not doing more about it, for rabbits invade his flower-beds and weeds spread from one part to another.

Lhota warrior (after Mills)

Throughout the century, there were constant Naga raids on the plains; head-hunting forays kept the Naga villages in a constant state of anxiety. In 1867, when the Gelati guard-house was attacked at night and some constables killed, there was much discussion about the reasons for these raids. Some thought that the encroachments of tea-planters in the hills were unsettling all the frontier tribes. Others considered that recent survey operations had excited their suspicions. Others thought that a prohibition to carry spears to market had upset them. But whatever the cause, the raids were serious. In 1851 no fewer than 22 were reported, in which 55 persons were killed, 10 wounded and 113 taken captive. From 1854 to 1865 there were 19 raids by the Angamis alone and 232 persons were killed, wounded or carried off. In the decade following 1874 six villages were plundered, nine wholly or partially destroyed and 334 people killed.

Official retaliation to these raids was usually severe. At one point the President in Council ordered that the 'most stringent and decisive measures in regard to these barbarous tribes' should be taken. The most common form of punishment was the total destruction of an offending village by fire which often caused loss to the innocent as well as to the guilty, and there are cases of completely innocent villages being burnt by mistake. Even worse, for houses of bamboo and thatch could quickly be rebuilt, was the destruction of granaries and crops. In 1866 a village called Razepemah, which had cut up a neighbouring Mikir village, was, in the words of the chronicler, 'levelled to the ground; its lands declared barren and desolate for ever; and its people were distributed throughout other communities.' Other forfeits took the form of fines of grain and cash and forced unpaid labour. In 1880 the village of Khonoma had its wonderful terraced cultivation confiscated and its clans were dispersed among other villages. The result was that the dispossessed villagers found themselves not only deprived of their homes, but, by the confiscation of their settled cultivation, they were during a whole year reduced to the condition of homeless wanderers, dependent to a great extent on the charity of their neighbours and living in temporary huts in the jungles. The result was widespread sickness and mortality.

Conflicting Policies

From a very early date there were two sharply opposed points of view about the development of the hills. Some officials, especially those posted in Assam who knew the realities of the situation, felt that Government should undertake a 'mission of civilization' and that the only way to prevent raids both on the plains and other Naga villages with their inevitable and distasteful consequence was to establish administrative control of the whole of India up to the Burmese frontier, occupy it in sufficient force, and go forward with schemes to ensure the progress of the hills.

An example of the Forward Policy is found in an important statement made by the Lieutenant-Governor of Bengal in 1866.

'The only course left us consistently with the duty we owe to the inhabitants of the adjoining frontier districts as well as to the Angami Nagas themselves, who are torn by intestine feuds for want of a Government, and unable to exercise any general self-control, or to restrain independent action on the part of any villages or even of a section of any of the numerous villages inhabited by the tribe, is to re-assert our authority over them, and bring them under a system of administration suited to their circumstances, and gradually to reclaim them from habits of lawlessness to those of order and civilization.

'These Angami Nagas are frequently mentioned in the correspondence of late years as independent Nagas, and a distinction is made between the tract they inhabit and British territory, as if the former was not included in the latter. But for this distinction there is no real ground. The treaties with Burma and Manipur recognize the Patkoi and Burrail ranges of hills running in a continuous line from the sources of the Dehing in the extreme east of Assam to those of the Dhunsiri in North Cachar as the boundary between those countries and British India. There is no intermediate independent territory, and while the wild tribes who inhabit the southern slopes of those ranges are subject to Burma and Manipur, those who inhabit the northern slopes are subject to the British Government. These latter, including the Angami Nagas, are independent only in the sense that the British Government has refrained from reducing them to practical subjection, and has left them, except at occasional intervals, entirely to themselves; but they have never enjoyed or acquired political or territorial independence; and it is clearly open to the British Government in point of right, as it is incumbent on it in good policy, to exercise its sovereign power by giving them the benefit of a settled administration.'

The other point of view maintained that, except for occasional military 'promenades' in the hills, the people should be left entirely alone. Although, up to 1854 some attempts at control had been made, in that year it was decided that troops already established should be withdrawn; and that punishment for raids should be mainly by stopping trade with the plains, for it was felt that the Angamis, for example, who had been discovered to be 'very intelligent and exceedingly anxious for traffic and gain', would be more influenced by this than by the rather ineffective burning of their villages.

Several different motives have been popularly attributed to the British authorities for their policy of 'leave well alone', one of the most ridiculous being that they wished to preserve the Nagas as 'museum specimens'. Although flattering to the artistic and antiquarian interests of what was in the main a rather unimaginative bureaucracy, this idea has no basis in fact. Nor did the British policy imply any suggestion that the Nagas were not included within India, which embraced everything up to the accepted border with Burma. There was only one reason why the British did not bring the entire area under active administration and control : it was too much trouble. It was also too expensive. An order of the Government of India in 1866 puts the situation clearly : 'Should the hillmen be gradually reclaimed to our rule and civilized, without much cost to the British Treasury in the process, it will be a good work well accomplished. But His Excellency in Council cannot admit that we are bound to attempt more in their behalf than the resources of the Empire can reasonably afford.'

Later, however, this policy of complete non-interference proved a failure. The Court of Directors had never liked it; 'it was too thoroughly English', wrote Mackenzie in 1869, 'to be appreciated by ignorant Nagas'; there were appeals even from the Angamis to intervene in their villages to prevent head-hunting. In 1866, therefore, an outpost was established at Samaguting and a school and dispensary were opened there. Roads were constructed down to the plains and trade was encouraged. Interpreters and messengers were appointed, trade increased and in one year three thousand Nagas visited the markets in the plains for peaceful commerce. A few years later, an official report declared that 'the name of Angami, once a terror to the peasantry of Nowgong and Golaghat and an abhorrence to civil officers, promises soon to designate as peaceful and industrious a people as any we have dealings with'.

The Establishment of the Naga Hills District

In 1877, it was at last decided to agree to the constant demands of the local officials that they should be given authority to act as arbiters in inter-village feuds with power to enforce their awards and in the following year Kohima was established as the chief administrative centre of the area, with a sub-centre at Wokha; a strong police force was posted in the interior; and a house-tax of Rs. 2 was taken. This was the beginning of an effective administration in the Naga Hills, which was established as a District in 1881. In 1888 a new sub-centre was opened at Mokokchung among the Aos.

The reaction of the Nagas to this arrangement was unexpectedly encouraging. Indeed, from a much earlier date there had been signs that, despite frequent conflict in some areas, an ordered administration was not altogether unwelcome. In 1841, for example, Lieutenant Briggs toured the hills and by bringing to bear what Mackenzie calls 'that nameless attraction which frontier officers are supposed, and often with justice, to exercise over uncivilized races', established friendly

PHOTO: P. PAL

THE DEPUTY COMMISSIONER'S 'BODYGUARDS' AT TUENSANG, 1960

PHOTO: S. SEN

AN ANGAMI VILLAGE GIRL

Village gate at Khonoma (after Hutton)

agreements with most of the leading communities and, at their request, opened a salt depot at Dimapur. In 1873, Captain Butler wrote of the Kutcha Nagas that this tribe 'would, I believe, be very glad indeed if the British Government would take over the active and actual control of their country, and protect them from the devastating attacks and extortionate demands of their more warlike neighbours the Angamis'. It was in fact only from one group of Angami villages that serious opposition came.

In 1879 the powerful village of Khonoma, which stands like a fortress rising above a valley surrounded by high mountains, showed hostility. The first Deputy Commissioner of the Naga Hills, Mr Damant, visited the village but he himself was murdered and thirty-five of the troops escorting him were killed. The Khonoma warriors besieged Kohima but in less than a week the little town was relieved from Manipur. In retaliation a strong punitive force was sent to Khonoma with the results which I have already described. After this there was very little disturbance throughout the District. There was a little trouble among the Semas and there was a serious inter-village feud in the Ao area, but from 1892 onwards it was only found necessary to despatch one regular punitive expedition in the course of fifteen years.

Head-hunting within the Naga Hills District boundaries (but not, of course, in the Tuensang area) quickly disappeared, inter-village raids came to an end and the Nagas settled down to a peaceful life of cultivation and trade.

The First World War

The First World War did not have any very great impact on the Nagas, though about two thousand of them were recruited for a Labour Corps in France. The Semas responded best, sending 1,000 men; the Lhotas sent 400, the Aos 200, the Rengmas 200 and, most significant of all, the Changs and other tribesmen of the then lightly administered area another 200.

There was also a remarkable response, considering the poverty of the people, to attempts to raise money for the War Loans, over twenty-six thousand rupees being subscribed to the first and thirty-nine thousand to the second.

The Second World War

The Second World War, however, had a more devastating and far-reaching effect. The Japanese penetrated up to Kohima and both the Naga Hills District and the Tuensang ranges saw the presence of many troops and suffered the dangers and disasters of modern battle. The Nagas gave invaluable support to the Allied forces and Field-Marshal Sir William Slim, in his book, *Defeat into Victory*, has paid a fine tribute to them, speaking of 'the gallant Nagas whose loyalty, even in the most depressing times of the invasion, never faltered. Despite floggings, torture, execution and the burning of their villages, they refused to aid the Japanese in any way or to betray our troops. Their active help to us was beyond value or praise.' 'They guided our columns, collected information, ambushed enemy patrols, carried our supplies, and brought in our wounded under the heaviest fire—and then, being the gentlemen they were, often refused all payment.' He concludes that many a British and Indian soldier owed his life to them, and 'no soldier of the Fourteenth Army who met them will ever think of them but with admiration and affection'.

The Tuensang Area

Precisely the same indecision that had confused the situation elsewhere later marked the policy of the British Government towards what is now the Tuensang District of the NHTA. Even after the Naga Hills District had been brought under ordered Government, the wild and rugged tract to the north-east remained. It was populated by martial tribes; there were no communications and no money to build or maintain them; and despite constant urging that it was inconsistent to develop one part of the hills and neglect another, the Supreme Government felt that until there were men and funds available it would be better to leave this territory alone for the time being.

The Government of Burma took the same view, declaring in 1895 that as long as the Nagas along their side of the border refrained from raiding the more settled Districts, there should be no interference in their affairs.

From 1902, under the provisions of a special Order-in-Council, the Tuensang villages were administered by the Governor-General of India through the Governor of Assam as his Agent and he was authorized to apply any British Indian Law to them. The Government of India Act of 1935 continued this arrangement, and Tuensang was defined as a 'tribal area' within India. There was no change in its status at Independence; the Indian Independence Act of 1947 and the Extra-Provincial Jurisdiction Act of the same year authorized the Government of India to continue its administration.

Even before Independence, however, Tuensang, beautiful and romantic, was by no means entirely neglected. At the beginning of the present century, the local officers felt strongly that some attempt to protect and develop the people was necessary and one of them wrote : 'Let the inhabitants clearly understand that they are British subjects, and as such they may look to Government for redress in return for the obligations we impose on them as regards raiding.'

From 1910 onwards there was a gradual extension of control, and in the next three decades there were a number of expeditions into the wild border hills to punish villages which carried out head-hunting raids into the fully administered areas as well as major raids among themselves. In 1913, for example, an expedition went to Chinglong and its subordinate villages, whose warriors had taken the heads of a number of Nagas at Wanching, and destroyed six villages : at least 120 Nagas were killed. In consequence a post was established at Wakching, in the Konyak country, where nearly a quarter of a century later Dr C. von Furer-Haimendorf was to spend a year in research, one result of which was the well-known book *The Naked Nagas*.

In June 1947 I toured for over a month in this part of the hills in the company of Mr W. G. Archer, a member of the I.C.S., who was in charge of Mokokchung. I saw how Tuensang was then divided into what were called 'controlled' and 'unadministered' areas, but how his writ did, in practice, extend over the whole area. Local Chiefs and headmen, who were called Command Dobashis and paid by Government, acted on his behalf and reported major incidents which required attention. From time to time punitive expeditions had to be taken out in serious cases of head-hunting. While I was in Wakching, many Chiefs in their gorgeous attire came from the most distant villages to have their difficulties and quarrels settled. During the last War it was possible to establish a wireless station here in a very remote village on the Burma border.

The North-East Frontier Agency

It must not be forgotten that there are many other tribes besides the Nagas in north-eastern India, and many of the problems of the Naga Hills are shared by them. In the great mountainous tract of thirty thousand square miles now known as the North-East Frontier Agency (NEFA), the British, apart from confirming the frontier with Tibet, followed much the same policy and for the same reasons, being content with a general supervision and control, the sending out of promenades and the appointment of special officers located in the foothills to settle those tribal disputes which were brought to them. Anything more, felt Government, would have been impossibly expensive.

After Independence, however, the strongly humanitarian instincts of the new national Government turned its attention, not only to the north-eastern hills, but to all the tribal areas of India, some of which were equally isolated and almost all equally neglected. On the frontier additional high-level officers were appointed, the administration was reorganised, and in 1950 the North-East Frontier Tract, comprising the Balipara Frontier Tract, the Tirap Frontier Tract, the Abor Hills District and the Mishmi Hills District, along with the Naga Tribal Area, was included in Part B of the Sixth Schedule of the Constitution, which I describe in detail later.

Four years later, the North-East Frontier Areas (Administration) Regulation 1954 provided that the Balipara Frontier Tract should be divided into two parts—the Subansiri and Kameng Frontier Divisions; that the other areas should be known as Frontier Divisions under the names of Tirap, Siang, Lohit and Tuensang respectively; and that these Divisions should 'be collectively known as the North-East Frontier Agency'. Tuensang continued to be part of NEFA until the end of 1957, when it was joined with the Naga Hills District to form the new Naga Hills Tuensang Area.

Far-reaching schemes of development were initiated from 1947; air-strips and roads were built; outposts for administration and development were opened.

I visited Tuensang in 1954 after it had become part of NEFA and toured there for seven weeks, covering some two hundred miles on foot. I found everywhere appreciation of the way the Government of India had taken over regular administration. The main feeling was one of profound relief that the burden of anxiety and fear had been lifted, for although head-hunting had not altogether disappeared and village feuds flared up from time to time, the people were now enjoying many of the blessings of peace. There was a constant demand for development, especially in the field of education and since my previous visit no fewer than seventy-three schools had been started and were being maintained at the people's own expense.

It will be interesting to examine how the District was opened up and why. Its headquarters near the famous and powerful Tuensang village was founded in 1948 as an outpost of Mokokchung and in 1951 the first political officer was appointed. Even before this an outpost had been opened at Longleh in the Phom area to control a situation which in those days was all too typical. In 1949 the village of Yacham had raided Kamaku and taken some heads. In December of the same year there was a dispute about fishing rights between Phomching and Urangkong, and Phomching took two heads from the latter village.

Five months later Urangkong retaliated, killed twelve persons in Phomching, took away eight heads and burnt half the village. The Deputy Commissioner of the Naga Hills District fined Urangkong twenty mithuns, the normal method of punishment, to be paid within twenty days. Yet before these days were over, Phomching, aided by four Phom and eight Chang villages, attacked and burnt down the entire village of Urangkong. The Deputy Commissioner took out a column to punish the organizers of the raid and after his visit the Phoms took an oath to stop fighting each other and at their request the outpost was opened to keep the peace.

Similarly, the establishment of the Kiphire outpost in 1951 was due to the fact that the Sangtam villagers here had lived for years under constant apprehension of attack from powerful Naga villages on the other side of the Burma border and they requested the Deputy Commissioner to establish an outpost for their protection and development. They wanted schools and hospitals and roads and offered to give free labour for their construction.

Another administrative centre was opened at Mon at the end of 1951 with the same object of giving protection to the Indian villages against Naga raids from Burma and to check head-hunting. In the same year an outpost was opened at Noklak in a very distant range near the Burma border which was constantly being attacked. During two raids in May of that year the village lost at least one hundred lives, of whom ninety-two were killed and their heads taken away, and eight burnt to death when their homes were set on fire. Fifty-seven of the dead were women and one hundred and eighty-one houses were burnt to ashes. As a result of this raid there was a conference with the Government of Burma at Rangoon and representatives of the two Governments visited the villages involved and imposed heavy fines.

North of Noklak the people were under the domination of powerful Burmese villages which used actually to decide cases arising between Naga villages in India. They also imposed taxes and constantly demanded money and cattle. As a result of the joint intervention of the Burmese and Indian Governments, the Indian Naga villages were freed of this burden, and in 1953 when the Political Officer of Tuensang visited the area they gave him a warm welcome and expressed their gratitude, declaring that 'they felt confident about the future as the Government had come to their land.'

In parts of the Naga Hills of Burma, human sacrifice, though generally checked by the Burmese authorities, continued to prevail, especially in the Haime area. There was some traffic in men, women and children from Indian villages near the border to villages on the Burma side, which in their turn sold them as slaves. As a result of co-operation between the Indian and Burmese authorities some of the slaves were returned to their villages during the year 1952-53. The Political Officer of Tuensang, during a tour of the Shamnyuyungmang area, dealt with cases of 15 persons, some of whom were children, who had been sold.

An Assam Rifles post therefore was opened at Pesou in 1952 to protect the Indian villages, prevent mutual raids and put an end to traffic in slaves.

Many other administrative centres and outposts were opened in the next few years and even today the people of Tuensang are asking for more in order that they may be able to live without fear.

The intention, therefore, of opening up the Tuensang area was primarily to solve urgent human problems, to give peace to the people and, with peace, to ensure the development of better communications, education, hospitals and improved agriculture.

The Course of History

There has been no space in this summary account to describe the Naga traditions of their origin or the speculations of scholars about their early migrations. Every tribe, sometimes every clan, has its own myths, tracing between them their first homes to every point of the compass. It has been suggested that their love of marine shells points to a bygone settlement near the sea; that their spears (with ornamental barbs curling outward from a shaft) suggest some relationship with the Igorots and the Philippine Islands; that they are connected with the Dyaks and Borneo through the common tradition of head-hunting, with Indonesia generally by the use of the simple loin-loom. This sort of thing is not very substantial evidence on which to build a history of ancient times, but it does give hints of what may have happened.

Undoubtedly the Naga Kiratas wandered far before adopting their present home. Dr Hutton concludes that: 'no Naga tribe is of pure blood. The tribes have combined elements due to immigration from at any rate three directions, north-east, north-west and south, the people having been pushed up from the plains of Assam and Burma by pressure. We may speculate that at a certain stage a Negrito race, later an Austric race of Kol-Annam or Mon-Khmer type was in occupation, leaving traces in implements and perhaps folk-tales now found. Then came a definitely Bodo immigration from the north-west or west, and by this perhaps the Y-shaped posts, reaping by hand and indications of a matrilineal system have been left. There is, beyond dispute, a mixture of Tai blood from the east also. The immigration wave from the south is obvious enough, and possibly brought up elements of population from southern Burma wedged in among migrating tribes. The Angamis are probably related to the Igorot and possibly other Philippine tribes by blood or culture or both. Further, these southern immigrants perhaps already consisted of two parts, one settled and cultured, the other barbarous but warlike; and the Angamis may have inherited certain customs from both parts of the tide. On the other hand it is possible that they contain some Aryan element from the other side of India caught up among migrating tribes.'

Even when we enter the period of recorded history the story of the Nagas is still obscure. There is a legend told by many of the hill tribes against themselves, that in the very early days God gave men skins of deer on which he told them to write their traditions. The people of the plains obeyed his command, but the hillmen, hungry and omnivorous, cooked and ate their writing materials, with the result that they were unable to leave any records of their past.

But we know enough to see the Naga tribes, and many other tribes too, winning from their heroic travels through the forests and over the hard mountains an exceptional toughness of fibre and physical strength. As they come into touch with other peoples, they are at first afraid, and (from one point of view) the history of the Nagas is the gradual overcoming of that fear. Their relations with the Ahoms brought conflict but it also introduced them to their first glimpse of a wider civilization. The slow encroachment of tea-planter, merchant and police on land which, if not their's, was at least their's to exploit, excited them to raid and battle, but gradually new opportunities of trade extending over a hundred years of commerce with the plains brought these widely different folk together. In their hills they fought one another and the menace of head-hunting cast a shadow on their lives, but in time this fear was lifted. The British often punished them, but they also made friends with them, brought order into their lives and helped to banish ignorance. The missionaries brought an ideal of gentleness and forgiveness. After Independence the new concept of a welfare state came to the Nagas, and the free Indian people took their tribal brethren everywhere to their hearts.

Seme Naga girl

The years went by; wonderful roads began to urge their way through the hills; the jungle was tamed and conquered; the masses of people experienced the essential sorrows and delights of all mankind; they tilled the forest clearings, they fished and hunted, they learnt new ways of doing things. Their sons and daughters went to school and the cleverest of them studied in India's universities and even abroad. Progress was hindered, peace impaired for a time when a group of politicians revived the suspicion and fear that had almost gone. But that peace and security is on its way back now, and in any case we must beware of estimating a people's history and the quality of its life by its dramatic and publicised incidents: a punitive expedition is not the final truth about Khonoma, the Japanese invasion is not the last word about Kohima. In spite of all set-backs, behind the suspicion and anxiety of recent years, the Nagas throughout the decades have grown in knowledge and freedom of heart—and this is the real point of Naga history.

III

INDIA AND HER TRIBES

To ANYONE concerned about the welfare of the twenty-five million tribal people of India the Constitution of the Indian Republic is a heartening document. Its first reference to them is in its Article 46: 'The State shall promote with special care the educational and economic interests of the weaker sections of the people, and, in particular, of the Scheduled Castes and the Scheduled Tribes, and shall protect them from social injustice and all forms of exploitation.' The Constitution is not content to leave this very fine ideal in the air, but goes on to lay down specific ways in which it can be implemented.

THE SCHEDULED AREAS

The first of these is a basic attitude which is very old, for an important feature of the historical policy of India, both in the British period and today, was the recognition that the tribal areas required special arrangements for their administration and development, and that some of them should not fall within the normal legislative provisions; indeed 'deregulationising enactments' existed from very early times.

The Province of Assam was created in 1874, and the Naga Hills District, which had previously fallen under the jurisdiction of the Lieutenant-Governor of Bengal, was included within it, and was placed under the control of the Chief Commissioner of Assam. Its administration was regulated by a number of Acts, the most important of which was the Scheduled Districts Act of 1874 which made special provisions for 'undeveloped tracts'.

A number of what were described as 'Scheduled Districts' were established (one of which, it is interesting to note, covered the whole of Assam, including Sylhet) and the Act empowered Government to notify what laws should be enforced in them. Before long, of course, Assam acquired the same legal status as the rest of India.

It was recognised, however, that the hill areas were on a different footing. They needed a much simpler, more personal and humane administration; the elaborate procedure codes were too difficult. The Frontier Tracts Regulation II of 1880, therefore, provided that a number of the border areas should be excluded from the operation of laws which might be considered unsuitable. One of these was the Code of Criminal Procedure, another the Civil Procedure Code, which in fact was never enforced in the hills; simpler regulations concerning stamps, court fees, registration and transfer of property, and techniques of administering justice in civil and criminal matters were devised. It was arranged that petty cases, both civil and criminal, should be dealt with by Village Councils, presided over by the local Chiefs and headmen chosen by the people themselves, with a procedure free of all legal technicalities, and to which lawyers were not admitted. Later, the system of Tribal and Village Councils developed considerably in the Naga tracts and the latest arrangements for village self-government in Nagaland are built up on the old and healthy traditions.

The Government of India Act of 1919 empowered the Governor-General in Council to declare any territory in India to be a 'backward tract'. This power was extended on a fairly large scale and by 1928, these 'backward tracts', which were distributed in five of the Provinces of British India, covered an area of 120,000 square miles and contained a population of over eleven millions. Within their boundaries, the Governor-General could direct that any Act of the Indian Legislature should not apply or only apply with modifications, and he could empower the Provincial Governors to give similar directions in respect of Acts passed by the local legislatures. Proposals for expenditure in these tracts did not have to be submitted to the vote, and no questions about them could be asked without the Governor's sanction.

The fact that the Naga area came under these regulations did not mean that it was separate from other parts of India or that its inhabitants were receiving treatment different from that given to other tribal people. In actual fact they were in the same situation as many millions of others.

Then came the Simon Commission and ultimately the Government of India Act of 1935. The Commission met some of the NEFA tribes beyond Dibrugarh as well as a large assemblage of Nagas at Kohima. 'No description,' says its Report, 'can convey to the reader the striking impression produced by these gatherings, or the difficulty of fitting the needs of such people into a constitutional scheme. These races must be among the most picturesque in the world, and until their energies are sapped by contact with civilization they remain among the most light-hearted and virile.'

The members of the Commission took exception to the word 'backward'—Sir John Simon (as he then was) is reported as calling it 'nauseating' and Mr Cadogan described it in the House of Commons as 'misleading'. 'It is true,' he said, 'that some of these tribesmen eat food which, if you or I eat it, would give us ptomaine poisoning at once, but you and I have no right to say that because a third person can digest food which we cannot digest, that person is, therefore, backward. It might be that his inside had reached a more advanced state of evolution than your's or mine, but it is a mistake to imagine—and I am speaking seriously—that, because their customs are different from our's, they are backward in every sense.'

Instead of 'backward tracts', therefore, the Commission proposed the establishment of 'excluded areas', of which there were two categories: Excluded and Partially Excluded. The principle of their selection was partly 'backwardness' but, even more, administrative convenience. There was a general feeling that all the tribal people needed some kind of protection but, as many of them lived mixed up and in close contact with other populations, this would not be practicable. But where there was an enclave or a definite tract of country inhabited by a compact tribal population it was classified as an Excluded Area. Where the tribal population was less homogeneous, but was still undeveloped and substantial in number it was classified as Partially Excluded.

The main point of distinction between these two types of area was that, while both classes were excluded from the competence of the Provincial and Federal Legislatures, the administration of the Excluded Areas was vested in the Governors acting in their discretion and that of the Partially Excluded Areas in the control of the Ministers subject, however, to the Governor exercising his individual judgement.

The reasons for excluding the main tribal areas from the general constitutional arrangements are given in the Commission's Report. 'The stage of development reached by the inhabitants of these areas prevents the possibility of applying to them methods of representation adopted elsewhere. They do not ask for self-determination, but for security of land tenure, freedom in the pursuit of their traditional methods of livelihood, and the reasonable exercise of their ancestral customs. Their contentment does not depend so much on rapid political advance as on experienced and sympathetic handling, and on protection from economic subjugation by their neighbours.'

The Commission continued with recommendations which, to some extent, anticipate arrangements adopted by the Government of India today.

'The responsibility of Parliament for the backward tracts will not be discharged merely by securing to them protection from exploitation and by preventing those outbreaks which have from time to time occurred within their borders. The principal duty of the administration is to educate these peoples to stand on their own feet. . . It is too large a task to be left to the single-handed efforts of missionary societies or of individual officials. Co-ordination of activity and adequate funds are principally required. The typical backward tract is a deficit area, and no provincial legislature is likely to possess either the will or the means to devote special attention to its particular requirements. Expenditure in the tracts does not benefit the areas from which elected representatives are returned. Moreover, the most extensive tracts fall within the poorest provinces. Only if responsibility for the backward tracts is entrusted to the Centre, does it appear likely that it will be adequately discharged.' In India at the present time large sums of money are provided by the Centre for the development of the tribal areas.

The Simon Commission recommended only a comparatively few areas for exclusion and the Government of India also displayed an anxiety to limit exclusion as much as possible 'both in its local extent and in its degree'. The British Parliament, however, as a result of the discussions which preceded the passing of the Government of India Act in 1935, considerably increased its scope. The question roused considerable controversy not only in the House of Commons but also throughout India. Sir Winston Churchill, who claimed in the House to be himself 'an anthropologist in his way', strongly criticised the principle of exclusion on the grounds that it was altogether inconsistent to put forward a Bill whereby the 'government of a mighty land' and such subjects as irrigation, police, revenue and so forth could be handed over to 'the new Indian bodies' who were expected to discharge their functions with perfect security in regard to them but were apparently incompetent to fulfil such a comparatively minor duty as the administration of the primitive tribes. He implied that it would be more logical to include in the scheme of exclusion 'the entire scope of the great Indian peninsula.'

Although after Independence the policy of 'exclusion' (under another name) was accepted and even extended by the Government of India, at the time it was regarded as an insult to Indian administrative ability and there were widespread protests and heated debates in the Indian legislatures, largely excited by some of the speeches in the House of Commons. Yet the Secretary of State for India himself presented the scheme with moderation, basing his argument on sociological rather than political considerations. The reason for exclusion, he said, was that 'these backward people will only be victimised if we try to impose on them institutions which, while they may be suitable for more advanced civilizations, will do nothing but lead to their exploitation. We realise the great danger of imposing upon them anything in the nature of representative Government as we understand it. We realise the great danger of imposing upon them criminal and civil codes, and all that is connected with them, which, while they may be admirable for civilized communities, are extremely dangerous and injurious to these backward races.' He added that it would be wrong to think that it was only English administrators who really knew about the tribal areas. 'Let me say,' he declared, 'in justice to many distinguished Indian administrators, that in recent years there had been developed a school of Indian administrators' who had specially studied their problems.

Other speakers during the debates stressed the dangers of isolation and urged that the scheme for exclusion should be only a temporary one. Earl Winterton, for example, said that: 'I believe far more in assimilation than in isolation. I do not think you want to turn areas into modern Whipsnades where you have picturesque survivals and where Englishmen are able to go out and say, "This is a most interesting ethnological race of people divided by 500 or 1,000 years from the rest of India."'

And Mr R. A. Butler, who was then Under-Secretary of State for India, said that 'while we do not for a moment deny the importance of special measures for these areas, if we have to choose between assimilation and segregation, we go on as before with assimilation. Segregation, we feel, may not in every case meet the proper desires and needs of such areas. Let us look to the future. If at this moment we decide on a ring-fence policy and segregate as many areas as we can, we put off to a later date the chance of assimilating the backward areas in the general polity of India.'

Unfortunately, the general tone of the debates in the British Parliament suggested that if the tribal areas fell under the control of elected

Indian legislators they would be ruined. Speeches contained such provocative statements as these: 'The only chance for these people is to protect them from a civilization which will destroy them and for that purpose, I believe, British control is the best.' 'It is not fair to put these tribes into the unrestricted hands of people whose object must be to exploit their labour and to sell them cheap goods at prices they are not worth.' 'They must not,' declared Colonel Wedgwood, 'be converted from good Nagas or whatever they are into bad Hindus.' Prominent Indian politicians 'have never displayed the slightest interest in this subject', as compared with 'Europeans who had a natural and strong sympathy with these people.' 'We are treating these backward tribes as though they were chattels who could be handed over either to the Indians or the Princes.' 'If they were taken away from direct British rule, their land would be alienated, and they would be recruited for the tea plantations and elsewhere'. There was altogether too much of this sort of thing, which not only offended Indian opinion in general but also, I suspect, filtering down to the tribes, and specially the Nagas, reinforced the idea that they would not get a square deal under an Indian Government.

I have dwelt at some length on the Simon Commission and the reforms that followed, for it was now that a really serious and far-reaching policy of giving special and separate treatment to the tribes was adopted. That the Government of independent India should have followed the same policy suggests that it was the way it was introduced rather than the policy itself which roused so much contemporary resentment in India.

As a result of these reforms of the nineteen-thirties, from the 1st of April 1937, the Naga Hills District, the North-East Frontier Tract, the Lushai Hills and the North Cachar Hills became Excluded Areas within the Province of Assam, and were thenceforth administered by the Governor of Assam acting in his discretion, though the executive authority of the Province extended to them. This meant that no Act of the Central or Provincial Legislature could apply to the Naga Hills District unless the Governor so directed, and he was empowered to make regulations for its peace and good government.

With the coming of Independence in 1947, the same arrangement continued, except that the discretionary powers of the Governor were withdrawn and henceforth he acted on the advice of his Ministers.

In the 1950 Constitution the Excluded and Partially Excluded Areas disappear, and their place is taken by Scheduled or Tribal Areas, while elaborate lists of communities to be known by the rather unfortunate expression 'Scheduled Tribes' were later notified in a series of Regulations. All the Naga groups are included among them and they receive a number of privileges and exemptions, especially if they are resident in the special areas.

The new Constitution, in fact, takes over the former arrangements but modifies them and enlarges their scope. Previously the emphasis had been on protection: now it was on both protection and development. After all, Sections 91 and 92 of the Government of India Act had done no more than exclude the areas concerned from the operations of the Legislatures and give the Governors certain powers. The Fifth and Sixth Schedules of the new Constitution are more detailed and specific.

The Fifth Schedule applies to areas and people throughout India; the Sixth Schedule makes special provisions for the hill areas of Assam. Let us glance briefly at the Fifth Schedule before considering the Sixth, which is the one that specially concerns us.

As in the Government of India Act, the application of laws is restricted, but whereas the earlier Act laid down that no Acts should apply to the specified areas unless the Governor directed that they should do so; under the new Schedule, laws will normally apply unless the Governor directs that they shall not do so. This is an important distinction, for it means that the exclusion is no longer automatic. Moreover the Governor now acts on the advice of his Ministers.

Formerly the Governor was authorised in a general way to 'make regulations for the peace and good government' of an Excluded Area, but now special attention is directed to the transfer and allotment of land, and the control of money-lending.

Before Independence, the scheme of exclusion did not in practice give much protection to the tribes, for too much was put on the shoulders of the Governors, who were after all very busy people. The Constitution, therefore, provides for Tribes Advisory Councils, three-quarters of whose membership will be tribal, and the Governors of all States with Scheduled Areas have to make an annual report to the President regarding their administration.

The Sixth Schedule

The hill districts of Assam came under a different arrangement, which is set out in a Sixth Schedule, and they are called Tribal (not Scheduled) Areas, and enjoy a certain measure of autonomy. This was possible because in Assam the tribal areas are much more homogeneous than elsewhere; few outsiders live in them; the people are more prosperous, and some of the tribes, such as the Khasis, Mizos and Nagas had, even by 1950, made singular progress in education.

This, however, was not so everywhere and the Schedule is accordingly in two parts. The Districts coming under Part A (which originally included the Naga Hills District) were chiefly distinguished by their District Councils; they had representation in the Assam State Legislature, to which they provided Ministers and Deputy Ministers; and their affairs came to some extent within the purview of the State Ministry, with the exception of a fairly large number of subjects reserved to the Councils and the over-all control of the Governor acting in consultation with his Ministers.

In Part B, however, which covered the North-East Frontier Agency and the Naga Tribal Area and, after it was constituted, the Naga Hills Tuensang area, the main provisions of the Schedule apply only potentially and will come into effect when the Governor, with the previous approval of the President, so directs. In the meantime the administration is carried on by the President, through the Governor of Assam, acting in his discretion, as his Agent.

The Sixth Schedule has been constantly criticised by the tribal people, but it does provide a basis for their education in self-government, and a measure of protection for them. The District Councils consist of not more than twenty-four members, of whom not less than three-fourths are elected on the basis of adult suffrage which means, in practice, that an overwhelming majority of local tribal people are elected and are in a position to control them. The powers of the District Councils include authority to protect the people's land, and place in their hands the management of all forests, except Reserved Forests, the use of canals and water-courses for the purpose of agriculture, the regulation of shifting cultivation, the establishment of village councils, the appointment or succession of Chiefs or headmen, the inheritance of property, marriage laws and social customs. Any laws made must be submitted to the Governor and receive his assent before they can become effective.

The Sixth Schedule also recognizes the importance of the traditional tribal councils and gives certain powers to courts established by the District Councils under the Code of Criminal Procedure. The District Councils also have authority to establish, construct, or manage primary schools, dispensaries, markets, cattle-pounds, ferries, fisheries, roads and water-ways and, in particular, may prescribe the language and the manner in which education shall be imparted in primary schools. A share of the royalties accruing from prospecting licences and from the extraction of minerals is to be agreed upon by the Government of Assam and the District Councils. Any disputes are to be referred to the Governor who will decide them in his discretion.

A very important provision gives the District Councils power to make regulations for the control of money-lending and trading by non-tribals. Even more important provisions lay down that no Act of the Assam Legislature in respect of any of the matters which I have mentioned above and 'no Act of the State Legislature prohibiting or restricting the consumption of any non-distilled alcoholic liquor' shall apply to any Autonomous District unless the District Council so directs. Furthermore, as regards other matters also, the Governor may, by public notification, direct that any of Act of Parliament or the Legislature of the State shall not apply to an Autonomous District, 'or shall apply to such District or any part thereof subject to such exceptions or modifications as he may specify in the notification.'

The Sixth Schedule, therefore, does give the tribal people of the hill areas of Assam a considerable control of their own affairs and protection of their land and customs. Had it been introduced in other parts of India, where the tribesmen do not enjoy anything comparable, it would have been welcomed enthusiastically. In Assam, however, the Nagas as well as the other hill people were already thinking in terms of a special State, for which, they felt, the Sixth Schedule was an unsatisfactory substitute. They wanted a Legislature and Ministers. What they got was a District Council.

Yet from the very beginning it was the intention of the Indian Government that if the provisions of the Sixth Schedule were found, in practice, to be inadequate, they would be considered for revision.

Other Constitutional Provisions

We have seen that in the last century one of the chief obstacles to the progress of the hill areas was the lack of money or at least a disinclination to spend it on what did not seem a matter of high priority. This was still a problem at Independence and Article 275 of the Constitution, therefore, provides that special funds shall be made available out of the Consolidated Fund of India to promote the welfare of the Scheduled Tribes in any State and to raise the level of administration of the Scheduled Areas to that of the non-tribal areas of the State, and very large sums of money are in fact now being provided.

In order to ensure that there is adequate tribal representation both in the legislatures and in the services, Part XVI of the Constitution provides for the reservation of seats in the Lok Sabha and the State Legislative Assemblies for members of the Scheduled Tribes. This provision was originally for a period of ten years but it has recently been extended for another decade. Article 335 lays down that the claims of the members of the Scheduled Tribes shall be taken into consideration 'consistently with the maintenance of efficiency of administration' in the making of appointments to services and posts in connection with the affairs of the Union or a State.

Finally, there is what we may call a scheme of inspection and control. It is laid down that 'the executive power of the Union shall extend to the giving of directions to any State' as to the administration of these areas. Article 338 directs that there shall be a special Officer, to be appointed by the President, to investigate the working of the safeguards which are made to protect the interests of the tribes, and Article 339 further directs that the President shall, at the expiration of ten years from the commencement of the Constitution, appoint a Commission to report on the administration of the Scheduled Areas and the welfare of the Scheduled Tribes; this has recently been appointed.

This, in brief, is the constitutional position of the tribes throughout India. A Constitution is something much more than a politician's promise or assurance; it means what it says and must be observed. Implementation may be tardy or imperfect, but this would be a recognized wrong which must be put right.

The Inner Line

What is known in India as the Inner Line Regulation has been the subject of many misapprehensions. It was enacted in 1873 in order to bring under more stringent control the commercial relations of British tea planters and others with the hill tribes. In Lakhimpur the operations of speculators in caoutchouc had led to serious complications and the spread of tea gardens beyond the fiscal limits of the settled territories of the time had involved Government in many conflicts with the tribesmen. The Regulation, therefore, enacted that no outsider could go without an official pass beyond a certain line that was drawn along the foothills of the whole northern and north-eastern tribal area—the line is by no means confined to Assam—and laid down rules concerning trade and the possession of land beyond it.

It was thus a twofold attempt to protect both the tribal people and the settlers in the plains. On the one hand it prevented encroachment on tribal land; on the other, by checking irritations that might incite the tribesmen to rebellion and raids, it protected the tea planters and their labour. It had nothing whatever to do with any ideological policy of isolating the tribal people, and it did not affect the sovereignty of the areas lying beyond it. It was clearly defined as being merely for the purposes of jurisdiction and the practical convenience of administration.

Since Independence, the Inner Line has enabled Government to ensure that planned contact and scientific development which countries all over the world have recognised as essential if tribal people are to be brought into the main stream of modern life without economic or psychological damage; and it has made possible the control of money-lenders, merchants and landlords who otherwise might have exploited them. Its principal aim was, in fact, not to isolate the people but to protect them from exploitation, and it is interesting that one of the demands recently submitted by the Naga leaders themselves is to retain its restrictions.

When disturbances broke out in the Naga areas, it was obviously necessary for Government to regulate the entry of visitors to ensure their own safety. Even so, in some cases foreign missionaries and others have been enabled to visit the hills from time to time and have received a warm welcome from both officials and the people. Responsible journalists visited the Naga area even in 1957; at the height of the troubles, a body of them toured Tuensang. Other newspapermen followed, one of them attending the Mokokchung convention. A representative body of journalists, both Indian and foreign, has recently at the invitation of Government, visited the Naga hills.

In other more peaceful areas beyond the Inner Line, there has been a large, though select, number of visitors in recent years; indeed NEFA, for example, probably receives more visitors than any other part of tribal India.

Mr Nehru's Policy

In addition to this, India's Prime Minister, who has always taken a profound interest in the tribal people and has a great affection for them, has frequently spoken about the spirit in which they should be administered and developed, and a few years ago he laid down five principles—a tribal Panch Shila—which should be generally observed.

(1) People should develop along the lines of their own genius and we should avoid imposing anything on them. We should try to encourage in every way their own traditional arts and culture.

(2) Tribal rights in land and forest should be respected.

(3) We should try to train and build up a team of their own people to do the work of administration and development. Some technical personnel from outside will, no doubt, be needed, especially in the beginning. But we should avoid introducing too many outsiders into tribal territory.

(4) We should not over-administer these areas or overwhelm them with a multiplicity of schemes. We should rather work through, and not in rivalry to, their own social and cultural institutions.

(5) We should judge results, not by statistics or the amount of money spent, but by the quality of human character that is evolved.

With regard to the Nagas, Mr Nehru's policy has remained unchanged for many years. As long ago as August 1946, a year before Independence, when he was President of the Indian National Congress, he said that 'it is our policy that the tribal areas should have as much freedom and autonomy as possible so that they can live their own lives according to their own customs and desires.' 'The whole Naga territory should be controlled in a large measure by an elected Naga National Council.'

'I see no reason whatever why an extraneous judicial system should be enforced upon the Naga Hills. They should have perfect freedom to continue their Village Panchayats and Tribal Courts according to their own wishes. Indeed it is our wish that the judicial system of India should be revised, giving a great deal of power to Village Panchayats.'

And finally he declared at this time that 'I do not want the Nagas to be swamped by people from other parts of the country who might go there to exploit them to their own advantage.'

Ten years later, in discussion with a Naga delegation which went to see him in New Delhi, Mr Nehru said: 'Not only is Naga territory their's but the whole of India is their's. It is their duty to build up their local area along with the whole of India, and preserve their customs and language within the integrity and unity of India.'

Speaking of Community Development projects, he said that: 'We do not mean to crowd your areas with outside officers: they are there only to train the local people. At the bottom we have a village worker, then the doctors, engineers and others. The whole idea is to retain the people of the area. This is the real great work we are doing in India today—to build up the people to produce their own leaders and not to thrust outsiders on them.'

To this the Nagas might reply: 'This is all very well. We have never questioned the attitude of the Prime Minister himself and we have great confidence in him. But what about all the other people in the Government of India and, in particular, what about the lower grade staff who actually come into our areas ? Can you really say that these hold the same views ?'

I would not suggest that everywhere in India the large number of tribal people are being administered in the Prime Minister's spirit. Even the provisions of the Constitution are still not fully implemented in some places. The virtual theft of tribal land, in spite of special legislation to prevent it, continues; millions of tribal people—and other people too—are still in the clutches of money-lenders and are still exploited by rapacious merchants. There are still, unhappily, officials and social workers who go into the rural areas in a spirit of superiority and condescension and who have a destructive influence on the people.

But during the thirty years that I have been working in the tribal areas there has been a wonderful change. Very genuine efforts are being made to protect tribal land, in spite of the fact that the tribesmen themselves are sometimes their own worst enemies in allowing it to pass out of their hands for some immediate advantage. Money-lending is controlled to some extent and alternative sources of credit are being provided, but there is still a long way to go. Training centres to inspire officials and other workers going into the tribal areas with a right attitude and techniques have been started and there are many officials today who have taken the Prime Minister's directives to heart and are trying to fulfil them in practice.

Nor is it only the Prime Minister who has voiced these ideals. The Home Minister, Mr G. B. Pant, whose Ministry is responsible for the bulk of the tribal areas in the country and who himself has the greatest concern for the welfare of the tribal people, has often spoken in the same strain.

Quite recently the Vice-President, Dr Radhakrishnan, has insisted that we should give up the 'big brother complex' in dealing with the tribes and should approach them 'with affection and friendship and not condescension and contempt.' He has admitted that Government is not satisfied with the progress made since Independence in the promotion of their political awareness or economic progress and has insisted that much greater efforts should be made to fight poverty, disease, hunger and ignorance. At the same time he has urged that 'the tribal people should not be exploited by uplifters and so-called moral reformers', and that they should not only be given complete freedom but should be encouraged to develop their own traditional arts and culture.

Successive Governors of Assam have advocated a similar policy and, with specific reference to the Nagas, the late Mr S. Fazl Ali, for example, said in a Republic Day message at the height of the disturbances that :

'The freedom that India has attained is ultimately in the best interest of not only India as a whole but of the Nagas themselves. This freedom is indivisible and has been embodied in an inviolable Constitution. Under this Constitution, our Naga fellow-countrymen enjoy equality of citizenship and equal opportunities with any other Indian national. The freedom is already there, if only it is understood aright and properly availed of.

'The great and diverse peoples of India, who have throughout campaigned against exploitation, coercion and domination, can be relied upon to uphold the traditions of freedom in all parts of India with their last breath. There is not the least desire on behalf of anyone for domination or exploitation. On the other hand, what is sought is fraternal co-operation and mutual prosperity. The Naga Hills being a part and parcel of India, we have always been prepared to accord to our Naga fellow-countrymen the fullest assistance and opportunities for development. Freedom in a narrow and fissiparous sense of the world is really no freedom at all, for it cannot then be concretely transformed into cardinal freedom, that is freedom from want.

'India has a message of peace and well-being for the whole of mankind and the cultural traditions of the diverse peoples of India are adequately safeguarded under the provisions of the Constitution. The Government of India aims at actively promoting the dissemination of the best cultural traditions and will stamp out human tyranny and violence under whatever pretexts these may be unleashed, for only then can the ties of fraternal cooperation be forged. Only through fraternal interdependence of our peoples can an all-round prosperity and progress be achieved.'

Ultimately, of course, the policy of India towards her tribes is the same as for all her citizens. Special arrangements were included in the Constitution for the tribes and other classes of people who had hitherto been underprivileged to enable them to make up ground that had been lost or never been possessed. This does not mean that they are to be regarded as a special race or type of human being; it simply recognises the fact that in the past they have, as a result of their remoteness and their simplicity, the fact that so many of them are inarticulate, been the kind of people who tend to get left out or forgotten. Since Independence, India has been trying to make up for centuries of neglect by a special concern and sympathy.

But this is for all the poor, for all those who have not yet had their share of the privileges and joys of life. The preamble to the Constitution of India declares that the Sovereign Democratic Republic will secure to *all* its citizens, including the tribes (the Nagas of course among them), the fundamentals of a life of freedom :

'JUSTICE, social, economic and political;

'LIBERTY of thought, expression, belief, faith and worship;

'EQUALITY of status and of opportunity; and will promote among them all

'FRATERNITY assuring the dignity of the individual and the unity of the Nation.'

PHOTO: AUTHOR

PHOM NAGA DANCERS, 1954

PHOTO: AUTHOR

A Konyak Chief's son

IV

YEARS OF CONFLICT

As far back as 1918 an organization called the Naga Club was founded in Kohima and Mokokchung. It consisted mainly of Government officials and leading headmen of the villages who used to come in for meetings at which social and administrative problems were discussed. The Nagas recognized very early that India would inevitably gain her independence and it is remarkable how seriously they prepared for the changes which they knew were on the way.

The Club ran a Co-operative Store in Mokokchung, one of the first to be opened in the hills, which still exists as the Ao Trading Co-operative Store.

When the Simon Commission visited Kohima in January 1929, members of the Naga Club submitted a memorandum to it demanding that the Nagas should be excluded from the proposed reforms and kept under direct administration to save them from being overwhelmed by the people of the plains. Their leader made the point that: 'You are the only people who have ever conquered us and, when you go we should be as we were'. The Nagas recall that Mr Attlee and the Hon. Mr E. Cadogan, who visited Kohima, smiled when they heard this.

It will be interesting to quote Mr Cadogan's recollections of this visit to Kohima which he gave in a speech on the Government of India Bill before the special Committee in the House of Commons in May 1935. 'I suppose,' he said, 'I am one of the few hon. Members of this House who have had conversation with the head-hunters of Kohima in their own jungle. These little head-hunters met us and had a palaver. Presumably the District Commissioner had informed the tribal chieftain that my head was of no intrinsic value as he evinced no disposition to transfer it from my shoulders to his head-hunter's basket which was slung over his back and was, I think, the only garment he affected. I am telling this to the Committee in order to prove that these little tribesmen are more sophisticated in their own particular way than perhaps the Committee may imagine. They have a very shrewd suspicion that something is being done to take away from them their immemorial rights and customs.

'This is the way they put it to me. They said, "We hear that a black king is going to come to rule over India. If that is so, for goodness sake"—or whatever corresponds to the expression "goodness sake"—"do not let it be a Bengali." They ended by saying that they much preferred Queen Victoria.'

There seems to be an impression that the members of the Commission were so impressed by the Naga claims that they made some special arrangement to exclude the Nagas from the proposed reforms. In actual fact, as we have seen, this was not so. There was no special arrangement for the Naga Hills District and the fact that it was classified as an Excluded Area simply brought it into line with a number of similar areas throughout the whole of India.

Morung with cross-beam roof

In April 1945, Mr C.R. (now Sir Charles) Pawsey established an institution, which was then called the Naga Hills District Tribal Council, with the aim of uniting the Nagas and repairing some of the damage done during World War II. In March of the following year this Council met in Wokha and changed its name to that of the Naga National Council (NNC). Its aim was to foster the welfare and social aspirations of the Nagas and it received official patronage as a unifying and moderating influence. Its original political objective was to achieve local autonomy for the hills within the Province of Assam and to train the people for self-government. It encouraged the Tribal Councils already set up by individual tribes and started others to administer their own local affairs and consider possible reforms. It published a small newspaper, the *Naga Nation*, for a few years.

At first there was no talk of separation from India, but the temper of the NNC began to change rather quickly and by June 1947 it issued an ultimatum that the Naga Hills should cease to be part of India when Independence was attained. There was a good deal of controversy on this point, for, in these early days, the Nagas were by no means decided on what they wanted. As one of their leaders has pointed out, 'While one group of Nagas favoured immediate independence, some moderates favoured the continuance of governmental relations with India in some modified form until they were sufficiently schooled in the art of running a modern State. There was a third minority which wanted to bring Nagaland into the position of a Mandatory State under the British Government for a specified period of time.'

Other suggestions came from abroad for the future of the hill areas in Assam. A former Governor suggested that a new State should be founded which would be in essence a Crown Colony quite separate from the Government of India; it was essential, he urged, that control should come from Whitehall and not from Delhi to ensure the Nagas a square deal. The United Kingdom, perhaps assisted by contributions from the Indian Government, would meet the expense. Sir Reginald Coupland proposed a rather similar plan which amounted to a condominium, suggesting that the Governments of India and Burma might have a treaty with Britain and that each should take her share of responsibility for the area. This idea was effectively criticised by a later Governor of Assam, Sir Andrew Clow, in 1945 and the Nagas themselves equally opposed it, though on other grounds, for they had no affection for any kind of colonialism and they proved as strong as any Congressmen in insisting that 'the British must go'.

The Hydari Agreement

In 1947 a delegation went to New Delhi to propose the extreme view, that the Naga hills should, at Independence, be left outside the Indian Union. Shortly afterwards Sir Akbar Hydari, a man of great sympathy blended with realism, the then Governor of Assam, visited Kohima and had a week's discussions with the Naga leaders. As a result of prolonged talks, a 9-point Memorandum known as the Hydari Agreement was drawn up. It was a short and simple document, though far-reaching in its effects. Its preamble recognised the right of the Nagas to develop themselves according to their freely expressed wishes. It went on to establish that all cases, civil or criminal, arising between Nagas within the Naga Hills should be disposed of by duly constituted Naga courts according to Naga customary law.

On the executive side, the general principle was accepted that 'what the Naga National Council was prepared to pay for, the Naga National Council would control'. No laws passed by the Provincial or Central Legislatures, which would materially affect the terms of the agreement or Naga religious practice, would have legal force without the consent of the Naga National Council.

Land with all its resources in the Naga Hills would not be alienated to a non-Naga without the consent of the Council.

On taxation the agreement was that the Naga National Council would be responsible for the imposition, collection and expenditure of land revenue, house-tax and such other taxes as might be imposed by it.

The then administrative divisions should be modified so as to restore all its forests to the Naga Hills District and bring as far as possible all the Nagas under one unified administrative unit.

The most important provision was Article 9, which ran as follows:

'The Governor of Assam as the Agent of the Government of the Indian Union will have a special responsibility for a period of ten years to ensure the due observance of this agreement; at the end of this period, the Naga National Council will be asked whether they require the above agreement to be extended for a further period or a new agreement regarding the future of the Naga people be arrived at.' The intention, of course, was that at the end of ten years the Nagas would be free to suggest, if they so wished, changes in the administrative pattern to suit their special character and to ensure a greater measure of autonomy within India. Some of the Nagas, however, misinterpreted the Article to mean that they would have the liberty to demand complete separation.

A year later, a delegation of Nagas called on the Governor to seek clarification whether the 9-point Agreement would actually be implemented. This was confirmed by Sir Akbar Hydari and Mr Bardoloi, the then Chief Minister of Assam, but they made it clear that Article 9 had never borne the interpretation the Nagas put upon it. There was no change of policy here : it was explained that the Article had always meant that after ten years more acceptable arrangements could be considered, if necessary, and a more developed system of autonomy worked out, but within the Indian Union.

The Sixth Schedule

Gradually the extremists gained more and more control of the Naga National Council. Naga officials had to withdraw from it : others joined Government service and thus left the field clear for those who favoured complete independence. A Sub-Committee of the Constituent Assembly visited Assam, including Kohima, and worked out the Sixth Schedule which I have described in the previous Chapter but in spite of assurances that the successor Government had no such sinister designs as were feared, that the Naga people would be treated as one with the rest of India and special efforts would be made to protect them from any danger of exploitation from outside, while at the same time they would be given full opportunities for development according to their own particular way of life, in a country whose very unity derived from a pride in the diversity of its cultural components, the Naga leaders decided to reject it and boycotted the elections which were held to constitute District Councils. This was really the turning-point. Henceforth, for several years, the history of the Naga area was marked, first by a policy of direct action and then by a carefully organised violent resistance.

Direct Action

The Nagas also boycotted the General Elections of 1952; no Naga sought election to Parliament or the Legislature of Assam and no Nagas exercised their right of voting. Government, however, went through—it had to go through—the full procedure of a General Election. Electoral rolls were prepared, election-booths were established everywhere, ballot boxes and papers were provided and Election Officers were placed in position. Yet there were no applications from anyone, no nominations from any side and no candidates to vote for. This caused the Nagas a lot of simple amusement and as a method of emphasizing their political desires was certainly effective.

In the next General Election in 1957, three Nagas filed nomination papers. There was no opposition and no voting and they were returned to the Assam Legislative Assembly, one of them becoming a Deputy Minister.

Wide support for the independence claim was sought by a plebiscite organised during 1951 when all villages were visited, signatures or thumb-impressions taken and oaths were administered in the tribal fashion to fight for Naga independence. The first technique of agitation was Civil Disobedience, which was no stranger to India, and the people began to refuse to pay house-tax or to co-operate with Government in, for example, development schemes or the repair of roads and bridle-paths; they forced official teachers to resign and children to leave their schools. They would no longer give labour or sell supplies to officials and police. Village headmen returned their red cloaks in token of resignation. They boycotted national and official celebrations.

The tempo of hostility gradually increased. Government employees, specially Naga employees, were threatened by posters and letters, denounced at meetings, sometimes attacked and killed. Some were kidnapped and held to ransom. Roads were damaged, bridges cut and official buildings burnt.

At the end of 1953, however, a Naga Goodwill Mission paid a fortnight's visit to other parts of Assam where they had a very friendly reception. The Mission's own report speaks of the atmosphere of extreme friendliness, the hospitality and the cordiality with which they were received. The Congress Party conducted the tour but gave the visitors every opportunity to meet members of other political groups, including the Bolshevik Party of Assam and the Communists, who did not, however, make much impression on them. At the same time, however, the Mission made many fantastic accusations against the Administration and, unfortunately, its visit did not lead to any definite result.

Frustrated by the failure of its boycott and attempts at negotiation, the extremists appear to have toyed with the idea of an armed uprising from some time in 1953, though the NNC never officially approved a policy of violence. The first plan was to infiltrate agents into the more recently administered villages in Tuensang and by mobilising the more virile tribes there, whose contact with the Administration had been shorter and where communications were more difficult, to set up a base for operations backed by the international frontier with Burma.

The Yengpang Massacre

The immediate result of insurgent propaganda in the hitherto politically innocent border ranges of Tuensang was the revival of head-hunting. Not far from the Burmese border there is a small village, Yengpang, which had an old quarrel with another village called Kojok. In 1936 the Yengpang people, who did not feel strong enough to attack their enemy by themselves, engaged the powerful assistance of Pangsha, a very common practice in those days, promising them a number of mithuns if they would raid Kojok. The Pangsha people did so and as a result their village was burnt in the punitive expedition that followed. Yengpang, however, was not punished, which annoyed Pangsha and they also failed to pay up the mithuns they had promised which annoyed Pangsha still more. They also cultivated part of the Pangsha land.

Naga memories are long. In October 1954 the son of one of the most important Pangsha leaders was ambushed and killed. The Pangsha villagers were not sure who was responsible for this and they first planned to raid another village, but this was prevented by the timely intervention of one of the local officials. Shortly afterwards, however, they learnt that the Yengpang people had performed a special ceremony to celebrate success in a head-hunting raid and they took this to mean that it was they who had killed their headman's son. Before news of their intention could reach the Administration, they descended on this much smaller and weaker village and killed fifty-seven villagers, including the local school-teacher with his wife and a small baby. At the time there were no officials and no security personnel anywhere in the area; and the incident was a perfectly normal act of revenge on the part of the Nagas themselves. In the past thirty years, Pangsha had been punished more than once for major head-hunting forays : now Government had to punish it yet again.

The Naga Federal Government

In March 1956 the insurgents founded what they ambitiously called a Naga Federal Government and its flag was hoisted on the 22nd of that month at Phensinyu, a Rengma village. As a 'government', this was somewhat defective : it had no mandate from the people; its members were neither elected nor accepted by the majority of the villagers; it had influence certainly, but its power was the power of autocratic force; its ideas were largely on paper and its organization quickly broke down. Its constitution, somewhat shortened, runs as follows :

'Nagaland is a people's sovereign republic. This has been so from time immemorial. There shall be a Parliament with a strength of 100 Tatars (M. Ps). The President will be elected by the people and his Cabinet will consist of fifteen Kilonsers (High Ministers).

'Nagaland will maintain permanent military neutrality. There will be no standing army for the maintenance of law and order. There will be a Department of Home Guards headed by a Chief to function in the dual capacity of police and patriot soldiers.'

This document was signed by a Kilonser, Mr Hongkhin, who is described as head of the Naga Government, and by the Chief of the Home Guards. Mr Hongkhin, the publication of whose name excited considerable surprise throughout India, was an elderly Naga living in a remote village near the Burmese border. It is said that some of the rebels approached him and asked him if he would agree to be President of Nagaland and, naturally flattered by this, he agreed. They then dressed him up in a European suit, put a pipe in his mouth and took his photograph. But, after doing this, they were tactless enough to ask for the suit back, with the result that the old gentleman's enthusiasm for independence somewhat declined.

Although it had little resemblance to any kind of democratic or representative government, the Naga Federal Government—as a revolutionary organization—was elaborately and carefully planned, and among its later declarations are these :

'All forms of trade, business, industry, transport and other public utility will be free and will be in the hands of private enterprise. Education will be in the hands of the people. Religion will be free.'

'In Nagaland, land belongs to the people and it will remain so. There will be no land-tax, and other forms of taxation (which Nagas have not paid before) will be formulated by different administrative units.'

'Each Naga village is a republic in its own right. Each Naga family or tribe occupies its own distinct region, and shall continue as before to exercise full authority over its own affairs, including land, community organizations, social and religious practices and customs.'

'Men and women, above 22 years of age, will have equal rights of voting. There will be equal wages for equal work, irrespective of sex.'

In addition to the Kilonsers and Tatars mentioned above, Angs were appointed as Governors of each tribal area and there were other functionaries put in charge of villages, Magistrates to preside over the different courts which were subordinate to the Federal High Court, Advisers who were called Ayazakipiu, Ambassadors, Deputy Commissioners and so on. Officials' names were taken from a number of different tribal languages. Thus, Kedahge which means President, is a Rengma word; Kilonser comes from the Yimchungrs, Tatar from the Aos, Ang from the Konyaks and so on.

At the same time an elaborate military organization of Naga Home Guards was established with a Commander-in-Chief. Each tribe had a division of five hundred men of all ranks under the command of a Major-General and the ordinary titles of the Indian Army from Brigadier to Sepoy were adopted. Regular uniforms were provided with the Indian insignia.

A section of the Naga Women's Society was very popular at first. Its duties were to act as nurses and cooks, make and mend clothes for the Naga Home Guards, provide receptions for VIPs visiting their villages, supply rations to those who had gone underground, procure medicines, collect information and work as couriers. From one village alone two hundred women volunteered for these duties. As time went on, however, the majority of them returned home, though Naga girls, some of them quite young, have always taken a strong part in rebel activities.

There was even a system of rewards and a Victoria Cross, a Military Cross and a Military Medal were awarded. The Home Guards were originally promised an emolument of Rs. 50 (a little less than £4) a month but this was never paid regularly and ultimately came down to Rs. 10 to Rs. 30 a month according to their requirements.

Great dumps of arms and ammunition were left behind after the Second World War, most of which the Nagas had hidden, probably for use in hunting. These were collected by the Home Guards and efforts were made to purchase arms and ammunition from Manipur and beyond Dimapur. Other arms were captured in raids on police stations and outposts. The Konyak Nagas had long been making guns in their own smithies and two three-inch mortars were manufactured so that some captured three-inch ammunition could be used. When Japanese supplies ran short the rifles were rebored to take .303 ammunition. Clothes and medicines were purchased in the plains from merchants who had no idea of the use to which they would be put.

A number of trained nurses and compounders, but not apparently any doctors, joined the movement and some elderly Nagas acquainted with natural herbal remedies proved of great value. A so-called Colonel who was shot through the stomach, a 'Brigadier' who lost a hand and a 'Lieutenant-General', whose fingers were blown off and who received grievous injuries on the body due to the explosion of a hand-bomb which he was cleaning, are said to have been cured by these tribal medicines.

The Course of Violence

Thereafter the rebels made an all-out effort to achieve Naga independence by an organized campaign of violence throughout the Naga Hills and Tuensang. Arson, loot, murder and intimidation of Government servants spread rapidly throughout the villages and soon proved beyond the resources of the Assam Police and the limited Assam Rifles force available there to control. Earlier, in the spring of 1955, the NEFA Administration had called in two companies of the Army for the special task of controlling violence in Tuensang, but released them later. By the beginning of 1956 the insurgent leaders had succeeded in building up an armed guerilla force of approximately five thousand men, which ultimately grew to some fifteen thousand, and in April of that year Government was forced to pass on the responsibility for operations against it to the Army which began moving in greater force into the hills. The rebels met the troops with violent opposition; they ambushed convoys on the roads and persistently sniped and sometimes attacked outposts. They continued their policy of attempting to terrorise Nagas who refused to help them and, by a device of mounting ambushes from the vicinity of villages, tried to involve the population as a whole in the inevitable counterfire and operations by the armed forces.

Although at first the rebels received a good deal of support, the village people quickly grew tired of their exactions of money, clothes and food which were often made at the point of a gun. Here was a form of taxation which they had never expected. From the beginning a number of villages had refused to support the cause and it was not long before the rebels met with a solid body of resistance. The result was that they adopted more and more violent measures to force those who were not co-operating to join them and to provide the supplies they needed. For example, a body of rebels attacked Pangsha village in 1955 but, although Pangsha had only one gun at the time, its inhabitants drove off this well-armed force with heavy casualties. The Nagas of Thevopesimi were less fortunate. The people of one section of the village refused to obey the rebels' orders and two hundred of the latter attacked them and killed all the able-bodied men, forty-eight of them, whose widows are now being cared for by Government.

Many other similar incidents occurred and finally a body of Village Guards was formed in response to the wishes of the people to organize themselves for the safety of their homes. Government supplied them with muskets, rifles and uniforms and gave them some training; in Tuensang, however, the Village

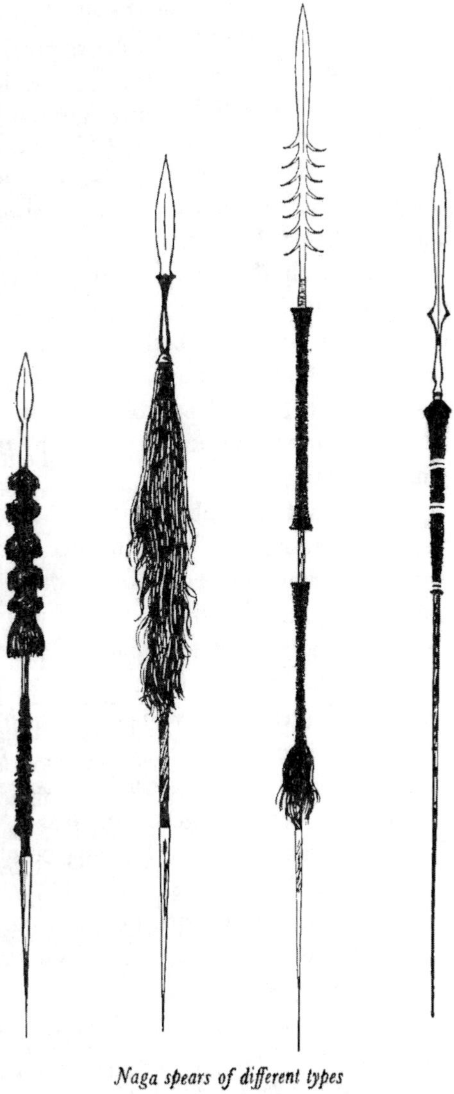

Naga spears of different types

Guards still wear their own dress. The Chiefs and headmen select the Guards themselves and have a large say in controlling their activities. They have on the whole been remarkably successful, especially when they are organized on a village basis and have been in a position to protect their own homes.

The rebels also turned their attention to the plains. Gangs of Nagas looted shops and kidnapped teachers; they raided railway stations and sniped trains; they made a serious raid into the Mikir Hills and even penetrated into the Khasi and Jaintia Hills. They ambushed traffic running between Kohima and Imphal. In a raid on Kachari villages on either side of the Dhansiri river, they completely burnt the houses, rendering some 500 people homeless.

Despite all this, the Government of India issued the strictest instructions to the Army that they were not, under any circumstances, to operate on a war-time basis, but strictly in aid of the civil power and at all times to use minimum force, never to think in terms of reprisals but rather to give all possible protection to the peaceful villagers. An Order of the Day, issued in 1955 by the Chief of the Army Staff, emphasised this:

'You must remember that all the people of the area in which you are operating are fellow-Indians. They may have a different religion, they may pursue a different way of life, but they are Indians, and the very fact that they are different and yet part of India is a reflection of India's greatness. Some of these people are misguided and have taken to arms against their own people, and are disrupting the peace of this area. You are to protect the mass of the people from these disruptive elements. You are not there to fight the people in the area, but to protect them. You are fighting only those who threaten the people and who are a danger to the lives and properties of the people. You must, therefore, do everything possible to win their confidence and respect and to help them feel that they belong to India.'

The Army did its utmost to carry out these instructions faithfully and its record is singularly clear of the conventional crimes of war—looting, cruelty and rape.

The conduct of the armed forces in general was rightly described by the Prime Minister in the Lok Sabha in August 1960. 'I think I can say with a measure of confidence that, on the whole, our Indian Army have functioned with discipline and credit to themselves and in accordance with their own high traditions.'

In all guerilla fighting, Security Forces—especially when subject to sniping and ambush—live under conditions of acute strain. Yet their behaviour was such that their relations with the vast majority of the people were friendly. The Assam Rifles, an armed constabulary which is part of the regular administration of the area, is a splendid body of men, most of whom are themselves Kiratas recruited from the hill people, who have guarded the mountains of north-east India for a hundred years. Their amiable and human approach, the way they often live under conditions which are, if anything, harder than those of the tribal people themselves, their courage and enterprise have made them very popular throughout the hills.

Army personnel too, who undertook their distasteful task with great reluctance, have done much to create a climate of friendliness by their genuine sympathy and many acts of kindness. It is now being more and more recognized that the Army went to the Naga Hills not to harass the people but, on the contrary, to protect them from harassment. Many Naga lives have been saved by prompt specialized treatment and advice from Army doctors, and some special Army medical units were formed three years ago to visit the villages and give aid to those in need.

Another important contribution to the general welfare has been the improvement of communications. The Pioneer Companies and the Army Engineers blasted rocks and constructed bridges at a time when no contractors or labourers were willing to take up the work, with the result that today jeeps can reach a very large number of villages. The roads are still subject to landslides and the Army Engineers are constantly engaged in clearing them away.

At a time when twenty-seven villages were in great need of food as a result of hostile action, Assam Rifles personnel shared their rations with the Nagas. Officers' wives have been running family welfare centres. During their patrols Army officers have paid attention to personal hygiene, sanitation and the general cleanliness of the villages and have certainly done a great deal of good. Other officers have been teaching Hindi, games and P.T. to boys in a number of schools; they join in their dances, appreciate their songs and music, share their food, encourage development schemes. Christian Army officers have conducted services in village churches. Some Army officers have been fascinated by Naga culture; they try to study it, and a young Army Engineer has written a full-scale book about it.

Christianity and the Nagas

From the days of the Rev. Miles Bronson, who in the forties of the last century, taught the Nagas Christianity and the art of cultivating tea, the missionaries were the pioneers of education and medical services. Mr Bronson started a few Naga schools and some of the Chiefs sent their sons to him for instruction. Another early missionary was the Rev. Clarke who came in 1876. In 1894 the American Baptist Mission opened their headquarters at Impur in the Ao Naga country and began their work of compassion and education. Unhappily, at the same time its representatives followed a culturally destructive policy, and robbed the Nagas of many of the things which gave vitality to their lives.

Perhaps for this reason progress was slow at first—there were only 211 converts in 1891 and 579 in 1901, but today at Impur there is a High School, a Bible School, a hospital and a central office and the majority of the Aos have been converted. In the great Church at Ungma, I recently attended a service which attracted a congregation of nearly three thousand people and at which the Deputy Commissioner preached the sermon.

The Naga Baptist Christian Convention is today organised into fourteen tribal associations representing all the major tribes of Nagaland. It maintains 632 Churches with a total membership of 73,500 persons. Each Church has a pastor supported by the local villagers who build him a house, provide him with food and pay him a small sum of about fifty rupees a month.

The Government of India has always taken a strictly neutral attitude towards religion and there is no interference of any kind in its practice or propagation, except that there are naturally rules that Government institutions, and especially schools, should not be used for proselytising activities and that Government officials should not give undue support to any particular religion. Such rules are inevitable in a multi-religious country like India, where official support of individual religions might lead to controversy and unrest.

When the disturbances began, there were vigorous—and successful—attempts to enlist the Churches on the hostile side. Many pastors took an active part in the movement, though whenever one of them did so the Church officially suspended him from his sacred calling.

Orders were early issued by the Naga military organization that every Company should have a pastor and it is said that most of the marching songs had a Christian motif. In 1956, an order was circulated by the Chief of the 'Country Guard Government of Nagaland' that 'God ought to be included in every practical field of Nagas and, therefore, as many pastors as possible should be appointed to prepare the war affairs'. Services were regularly held in the various hide-outs and there was a great deal of propaganda that since Nagaland was to be the first completely Christian State in Asia (today Naga Churches are placarded with posters saying 'Nagaland for Christ') it was the duty of Christians to fight the 'Hindu Government' in order to preserve their religion.

Vigorous counter-action was taken by some leading pastors and once the Naga Christians realized the protection given by the Constitution not only to practise one's religion but to propagate it, they accepted the view that on religious grounds they could certainly find a home in India, and many of them withdrew from the hostile movement.

Unfortunately, since the rebels often made their attacks on the Security Forces from the neighbourhood of villages, it was inevitable that in a number of cases these should have been burnt down and a few Churches were accidentally destroyed, though great care was always taken to spare them. In such cases Government has provided funds to restore the buildings.

There were half a dozen foreign missionaries in the Naga Hills District in 1947. One died, another left India on personal grounds, two other were transferred to other spheres of work, but only two were asked to leave the area as there was evidence that they had interested themselves in political matters in contravention of the conditions under which they had been permitted to enter the country. There is one missionary, an Italian, at present in Kohima.

The Nagas themselves, however, feel today that they are capable of running their own Church without the aid of foreign missionaries and, in fact, they are doing very well and their own Naga missionaries are proving far more successful than outsiders. For theological and pastoral training they are sent to mission stations in the plains.

Some American missionaries, who visited the Naga area last year, declared that in all their experience they had not come across a place where Christians had greater freedom and were making such striking progress. Three other American Baptist missionaries, who visited Mokokchung and Ungma on their way through India on their return from a World Conference in Rio in July 1960, gained a similar impression. There has been no interference with the activities of the Naga clergy who have held conventions of several thousands of Christians, have established churches on a very wide scale, and have had complete freedom to preach and teach so long as they have kept clear of politics. Some Christian officials (including officers of the Army) have preached in the Churches and have guided and helped the Nagas to revive some of their old traditions adapted to Christian needs. For example, there is great scope for the Nagas to use their traditional instinct for wood-carving in the decoration of their churches; hand-woven cloth is now sometimes being used; and last year there was a great procession on Easter Day in Kohima of Nagas in all their traditional finery.

Until recently, two out of the three Deputy Commissioners in the NHTA were Christians and the third was a Parsi. Over two thousand Naga and other Christians are employed in the administration of the Naga areas.

The Rise of Naga Liberalism

From the beginning a strong section of the Naga population had recognised that the demand for separation from India was unrealistic and that a campaign of violence was futile. As hostilities intensified during 1955, some of the Naga leaders decided that something would have to be done to change the course of events: they held a meeting in Khonoma and a number of them resigned from the NNC. Mr T. Sakhrie, whom I quote more than once in this book, was among them. One night in January 1956, his house was surrounded by a large party of rebel Nagas: he was taken out and led away into the forest, where he was tortured and killed.

From this time onward, the liberal leaders, at great risk to themselves, began to assert themselves more and more and came out openly to condemn the hostile movement. The Government of India, on its side was constantly exercised by the desire to terminate the unhappy situation as quickly as possible. In September and October 1956 the Prime Minister met delegations of Nagas at Delhi and Shillong and assured them, as he had assured them before, of Government's intention to grant them maximum autonomy. But his condition was that violent attempts to achieve this must cease before any political settlement could be considered.

The Liberal leaders at first thought mainly in terms of bringing violence to an end; it was only later that they began to consider a realistic political solution.

A Naga Peace Organising Committee was formed in 1956 and appealed to the people to abandon the policy of armed force.

In early 1957 for the first time the Church and its ministers came forward to condemn violence, and they issued an appeal at Kohima urging the Christian Nagas to work for peace; a meeting of 500 Church delegates at Impur made a similar declaration.

In the summer of 1957 the Nagas convened an All Tribes Naga Peoples' Convention in Kohima. This was held from the 22nd to the 26th August 1957 and was unique in Naga history for its representative character. There were 1,765 delegates and over 2,000 visitors representing every tribe. There are reasons to believe that the rebels gave tacit support to this move, though they did not actually take part in the Convention. The first resolution advocated a negotiated settlement of the Naga problem and the third suggested that, pending a final political solution, the present Naga Hills District of Assam and the Tuensang Frontier Division of NEFA should be constituted into a single administrative unit under the External Affairs Ministry.

The Naga Peoples' Convention (NPC) was now founded and its leaders were hopeful that the insurgents would come overground to join them. They, therefore, declared that the resolution passed in the Convention should be considered only as an interim demand and the final political settlement should wait till the extremist leaders joined hands with them in carrying out further negotiations with the Government of India.

The essential importance of this meeting was that for the first time after the troubles began, a large body of Nagas declared their opposition to violence, and adopted constitutional means to achieve their political object.

After the Convention, a nine-man Delegation met the Governor of Assam in Shillong, and later the Prime Minister in New Delhi, to present their resolutions.

As a result a separate administrative unit known by the clumsy name, Naga Hills Tuensang Area (NHTA), under the Ministry of External Affairs of the Government of India and administered through the Governor of Assam acting in his discretion as the Agent of the President, was brought into being from the 1st December 1957.

It was divided into three Districts—Kohima, Mokokchung and Tuensang, each in charge of a Deputy Commissioner, with a Commissioner at Kohima in over-all control and responsible, through the Adviser, to the Governor.

At the same time, and in order to create a proper atmosphere for the new Administration to function, an amnesty was declared and orders issued for the release of convicts and undertrial persons for offences committed against the State.

The constitution of this new administration gave an impetus to those who had lost faith in violence and the suffering it inevitably brought. Large numbers of rebels came overground until finally the figures swelled to nearly 3,000 who surrendered, 3,000 more who came voluntarily overground and returned to their villages, while a total of some 4,000 were arrested, most of them being released under the terms of the amnesty.

In the interior many villages held meetings to denounce the extremists. There was constantly increasing co-operation with Government in schemes for development, even though armed troops sometimes had to guard, for example, Community Development Block headquarters. Schools were re-opened. National festivals, such as Republic Day, were observed with a new zest, and from 1958 the celebrations have been on a large scale at all the District headquarters.

A second Naga Peoples' Convention was held in Ungma, a very

Street in Ungma village (after Mills, 1926)

large village near Mokokchung in May 1958. Ungma was chosen as the venue of the Convention, because apart from being one of the most notorious pro-hostile villages, the Aos claimed that the active resistance to Government authority which led to violence began there. The rebels threatened the villagers that they would impose a fine of Rs. 50,000 if they allowed the Convention to be held, but in fact between 150 and 200 themselves were present.

The NPC leaders hoped that the underground leaders would eventually co-operate with them on a united all-Naga basis in drafting acceptable proposals for a final settlement and, therefore, appointed a Liaison Committee to contact them and try to win them over.

The importance of this was obvious, for later, after the demand for Nagaland had been accepted, hostile pastors used the story of the Golden Calf in their propaganda. It was recalled that, while Moses (symbolising the rebel leaders) was away in the mountains receiving the Ten Commandments at the hands of the Lord, the Israelites, weary of the privations of the wilderness, went astray and created and worshipped the Golden Calf (of a State within the Indian Union). Everyone who had a Bible could read, in Exodus XXXII, what happened then!

But the attempt to win over the hostile leaders failed, and the Ungma Convention therefore had to be content with the appointment of a Drafting Committee to formulate their constitutional demands, but they were insistent at the same time that Government should leave the door open for the underground leaders to join them in the task of drafting it if they wanted to.

The Drafting Committee, which included a former Kilonser or Minister of the underground Government and a number of former rebel leaders, prepared a 16-point Memorandum for the constitution of a separate State to be known as Nagaland within the Indian Union.

A third meeting of the Naga Peoples' Convention was accordingly held at Mokokchung in October 1959. This turned out to be a great occasion. Thousands of people attended, and the little town put on a festive appearance; never before in its history had so many colourful shawls worn by different tribes been seen together at the same time. Women poured in to sell vegetables, eggs and meat, and prices shot up. Every house was full of guests and the few hotels were crowded with people discussing their future. There was an air of excitement and hope.

The main demand formulated by the Nagas at this Convention was for the constitution of a separate State within the Indian Union to be known as Nagaland, under the Ministry of External Affairs, with a Governor and administrative secretariat, a Council of Ministers and a Legislative Assembly. Provision was also made for the constitution of Village Councils, Range Councils and Tribal Councils to deal with matters concerning different tribes and areas, which would settle—among other matters—disputes and cases involving breaches of customary laws and usages.

A number of special resolutions were appended to the 16-point Memorandum. One records its appreciation of the Administration's concern for welfare activities and the progress made in the administration of the area. Another makes a request for the extension of the amnesty, such as the release of Naga political prisoners, a general pardon to the underground people coming overground, the relaxation of military patrolling and operations and any other restrictions, so as to promote free contact between the overground and underground people during the amnesty period.

Mokokchung village thirty years ago (after Shakespear)

A significant resolution of the Convention is as follows:

'The Naga Peoples' Convention further appeals to the Naga people in general and the aggrieved families in particular to extend the same general pardon to the underground people coming over-ground and also we appeal to all underground Nagas to stop all sorts of violent activities from now on.'

The Convention also asked for the co-operation of every tribe to bring the situation back to normal, and invited the underground people to participate fully in the running of the new Government of Nagaland.

A delegation of NPC leaders met the Governor of Assam in Shillong for preliminary discussions in April 1960 and would normally have proceeded soon afterwards to Delhi. The Prime Minister, however, was greatly preoccupied with riots in Assam, a General Strike and a visit abroad and it was not possible to arrange for the Naga leaders to present their case to him until the end of July, when the Government of India at this historic meeting vindicated its traditional stand and the principle of a Naga State, to come into being after a transitional period which the Nagas themselves desired, was accepted.

Ao Naga textile design

V

SUSPICION AND ANXIETY

The Naga disturbances are unique in having an almost entirely political foundation. During the British period there were many tribal rebellions throughout India for, as Dr J. H. Hutton, himself a member of the Indian Civil Service, has said, 'far from being of immediate benefit to the primitive tribes, the establishment of British rule in India did most of them much more harm than good.' Although many British officers regarded the tribes with great sympathy, they did little, perhaps they were not in a position to do more, to protect or help them, and with the advance of a co-ordinated and powerful administration and the opening up of tribal territory, the alienation of tribal land, the gradual deprivation of tribal rights in forests and the invasion of large numbers of money-lenders and merchants brought about the economic and psychological downfall of many of the tribes. The introduction of police, some of whom were sent into the tribal areas as a punishment for misbehaviour elsewhere, sometimes produced situations which drove the tribesmen to despair and rebellion.

Many of these revolts, such as the Ho, Munda and Uraon, were due to the loss of land. The Santal rebellion in 1855 is said to have been excited by economic loss caused by grasping and rapacious money-lenders and a system which permitted personal and hereditary bondage for debt; the unparalleled corruption and extortion of the police; the impossibility of the Santals obtaining redress from the Courts; the ignorance of tribal customs and indifference to tribal needs on the part of the administrators of the day; and the expropriation of Santal land. The Koya rebellion in East Godavari in 1879 has been traced to the behaviour of the police. The Kol insurrection of 1833 was mainly caused by the encroachment of alien farmers. The Saora troubles in 1941 were due to the imposition of new forest laws.

All these revolts had definite and recognizable causes which could be diagnosed and cured and, when better conditions were obtained, the people settled down happily. There have been few such disturbances since 1947, though various tribal groups have started political agitations for separate administrations or States within India.

Had the Nagas suffered wrongs comparable to those endured by the Santals and other tribes, it would have been possible to redress them. In the ten years following the end of the Second World War, however, it was rather suspicion and fear about what was going to happen than anything which actually had happened that roused anxiety in their minds, and it is essential that we should understand how this came to be. For we must not look on the Nagas as barbarians intolerant of any civilised control or as head-hunters only partially reformed; they are a fine people, with a civilization of their own, an ethic that works, hopes and desires for the progress of their land, a strong pride of race, which they share with many other tribes throughout India, and a passionate concern to protect their own lands, forests and way of life from outside interference.

The Fear of Change

At this time, not only the Nagas but all the tribes of Assam suffered from a sense of anxiety and fear of change, and the other tribes also formed political organisations such as the Garo National Council, the Khasi Federation, the Mizo Union and the United Mizo Freedom Organization in the Lushai Hills, for the preservation of their tribal way of life.

The situation then has been eloquently described by the Naga writer, the late Mr T. Sakhrie—and we should listen to the Nagas themselves whenever we can.

'Up to the time of the Japanese invasion in 1944 the Nagas had lived in an age of almost uninterrupted continuity with the past. The Nagas made a leap, as it were, from a distant past into the glare of the present century with the advent of the Japanese and found their world greatly changed. They looked about with uncertainty and pinched themselves to be reassured that all this was really true. Prior to the War, except in the case of the Aos, school-going was still unpopular and looked upon as a necessary evil which had to be put up with somehow. Suddenly they found themselves clamouring for more and more schools in which they saw social progress and, where Government could not build them, they went ahead to build their own. Existing schools were filled to overflowing.

'People became suddenly restive with the existing state of affairs. There was social unrest, economic unrest, political unrest. Everywhere there were cries of better, bigger and nobler things. Things that were considered a luxury became the standard of the day. Trade received a new impetus, as indeed the era brought in a new impetus to all fields of human endeavour. Two hundred miles of motorable road were added to those which had existed from before the war.'

Standards of value and taste often changed. 'Foreign dress which, before the war, had been considered a luxury but in good taste, had to yield place to the artistic native dress on which the new nationalism had stamped its approval. Foreign culture had to make way for the native culture. National dances and native songs were restored to their original places of honour. The clans which used to emphasise their differences hastened to patch them up and forged their unity. The clash of imperialistic interests had given birth to the new era—full of opportunities and hopes for a glorious future.'

The Naga Temperament

Another factor of great importance is the Naga character or temperament. The Nagas are by nature singularly free and independent, scornful of control, impatient of criticism. Nearly everyone of them has behind him a long history of life in a village at war with its neighbours, a tradition of adventure and courage.

Their 'man-to-man' attitude, which we must admire, may be illustrated by two incidents in the past. In 1855 Major Butler described how two Naga 'heralds' came to his camp.

'After seeing our muskets and guns, they scornfully declared they did not care for our *choongas* (tubes) meaning muskets. "Your Sipahees are flesh and blood as well as we", and they added, "we will fight with spear and shield, and see who are the best men: here is a specimen of our weapons", handing over a handsome spear.'

An expedition to punish a head-hunting raid spent Christmas Day 1909 at Tuensang, and the local people have long preserved a tradition of what happened. The first demand of Government, they remember, was for the men responsible for the outrage. To this the Tuensang people replied, 'Does a hunter give away his hounds?' The next demand was for a fine in money. To this the reply was, 'We have no coins. We hear the Government makes coins. If they are short, let them make some more.' The final demand was for mithuns, the customary fine for head-hunting in British days, to which no reply was given, but the animals were quietly tied up outside the village gates.

PHOTO: AUTHOR

THE OLD WORLD: THE DAUGHTER OF A KONYAK CHIEF, PHOTOGRAPHED IN 1947

PHOTO: S. SEN

THE NEW WORLD: AN ANGAMI GIRL OF TODAY

The Basis of the Naga Attitude

I have explained at some length the general policy of India towards her tribes and her specific policy towards the Nagas. Let us, therefore, examine, on the other side, the basis of the Naga attitude. Fundamentally, this comes down to three propositions. 'Nagas are not Indians and do not want to become Indians'. 'Naga territory is not, and has never been, a part of the Indian territory'. 'Nagaland was never conquered by India. It was conquered by the British and once the British left India it should revert to its original free status.' 'The Nagas are determined to have complete independence. They are determined not to join the Union. They will all die before losing their independence.'

This is the fundamental stand of the Naga extremists and it has nothing to do with any grievances that may have accumulated in recent years, for it was held by them even before India was independent.

Naga Propaganda

As time went by, however, the propagandists of the Naga National Council developed an expert publicity department directed until the end of 1955 by the capable and expert Mr Sakhrie, and later by others who had learnt the technique from him. Naga propaganda has often in fact been quite brilliant, carefully adapted to the psychology of the people, and in sharp contrast to the dull and pretentious publicity work of Government.

Its first aim was to intensify the deep-rooted natural Naga love of a free and uncontrolled life. A Naga recently spoke to me of 'independence' as the sweetest word that ever came from human lips. It was not difficult to rouse the people, especially in the Tuensang area which had so recently come under administration, with the idea that their freedom would gradually be taken from them and even the fact that they were no longer able to practise head-hunting as before was used as a propaganda point against the Government.

An idyllic picture, somewhat divorced from reality, of what a free Nagaland was like, was created. Mr Sakhrie himself, for example, wrote:

'Truly we are a peculiar people. We are all equals. Men and women have an equal social status. We have no caste distinctions; no high or low class of people. There is no communal feeling, neither are there religious differences to disturb our harmony with our conditions. There is no minority problem. We believe in that form of democratic government which permits the rule, not of the majority, but of the people as a whole. We govern ourselves by a government which does not govern at all.

Drinking-mug

'In the life of the village the family is a permanent living institution, a conscious unit in the national polity. Every family is proud of its own and no family has ever been left by their fellowmen to the mercy of circumstances. Possessing its own house, built on its own land, no family ever pays any tax. Forests and woodlands, rivers belong to the people for their exploitation without paying taxes. We cultivate as much land as we need or desire and there is no one to question our rights.

'We have food to eat and drinks to drink exceedingly above our needs. Truly God has been good to us. Three square meals a day and *zu* (rice-beer) without measure. We have no beggars.

'Every family lives in its village in its own right. It has no landlord to harass it, and no revenue collectors to knock on its door; for the family is the master of its own affairs.

'And, wonder of wonders, we have no jail. We do not "arrest" nor ever "imprison" anyone. Our civil authority is God in the matter of life and death. And murder is very rare.

'We fear nobody, individually or collectively. We are a healthy people and fear corrupts the health of man. What peace we have, no police, and no CID! We use no locks. Our granaries are kept outside the village and no guard is ever needed, for there is no one to steal from them. We travel as we like and it costs nothing. Wherever we go, it is our home. If by ill-fortune, a man falls sick or dies, he is borne home to his family without counting the cost.

'We talk freely, live freely and often fight freely too. We have no inhibitions of any kind. Wild? Yes. But free. There is order in this chaos; law in this freedom. If I were to choose a country, it would be Nagaland, my fair Nagaland—again and again.'

Another matter on which the Naga propagandists laid a great deal of stress was taxation. The villagers were told, in the words of a booklet issued at the end of 1953, how 'in the plains, unlike our Naga country, land belongs to the State and the people have to pay taxes for land, for house-sites and buildings too, for fisheries and even for forest products. They have a water tax, latrine tax, entertainment tax, road tax. Everything has to be paid for if they want to live in this world. We Nagas pay no tax. We have fisheries over 400 miles of river in which the people catch fish throughout the year, paying nothing. There are many forms of taxes that our people may not consider it wise to pay just to follow others: yet, change is bound to take place.' The Naga propagandists warned the people that the Government of India would soon be taxing their land, livestock and income and that the former happy state of affairs would soon disappear.

The problem of how to obtain money for a separate State did not seem to bother anyone and the rebels would point to a clump of bamboos and say, 'Here is our wealth', or would strike the ground and declare, 'The earth herself will provide us with all we need. Here are oil and minerals'. The general idea was that the future Naga Government would be run on very little money, since the Nagas would show their patriotism by working for practically nothing, as indeed many school-teachers and pastors already work for a mere pittance. Counter-arguments about 'viability', therefore, did not have much effect.

In the more advanced areas, especially in Mokokchung, there was a definite attempt to win over the churches by warnings that the 'Hindu Government' of India would soon put an end to Christianity and would force the Nagas to become Hindus, and for a time many Christians, who were ignorant of the protection given to their religion in the Constitution, became alarmed and joined the insurgents.

Another matter on which the rebel leaders laid considerable stress was the promise of foreign aid. In the Tuensang area, for example, so completely did some of the tribesmen believe that corrugated iron sheets would be sent to everyone whose house was burnt in the

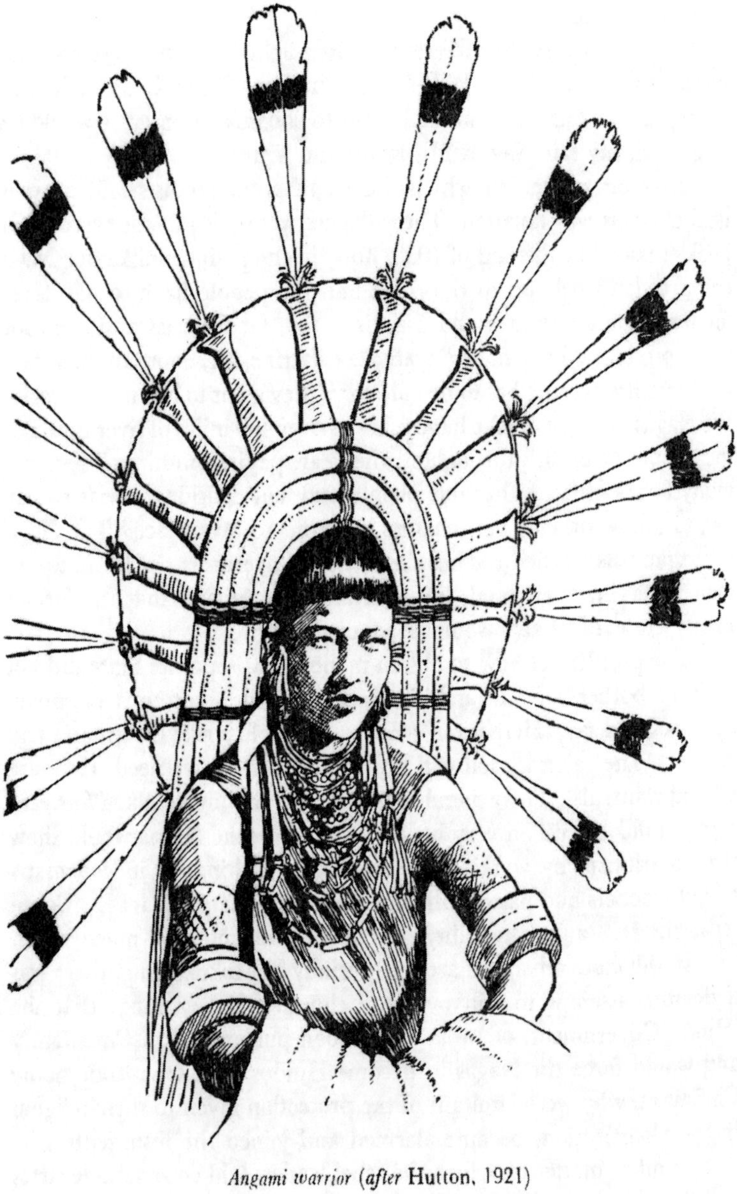

Angami warrior (*after* Hutton, 1921)

disturbances, that some of them actually burnt their houses themselves in the hope that they would get this benefit.

The Nagas are very fond of meat, and they were told that India would certainly stop beef-eating; this idea gained strength from the Cow Protection movement. They are also very fond of rice-beer and, in spite of the provision in the Sixth Schedule that there would be no interference in this, many were easily persuaded that India's prohibition policy would one day be applied to them. The grant of a licence for oil exploration was interpreted as likely to lead to exploitation of Naga land.

The rebel publicity agents adopted themselves very cleverly to local circumstances. The great Konyak tribe is divided into two sections, one of which lives under the autocratic rule of powerful Chiefs while the other is more democratic. The rebels told the Chiefs that the Indian Government would very soon take away their powers, and thus enlisted a number of them on their side. At the same time they told the democratic villages that the Government was proposing to institute the system of Chiefs who would take away their liberties, and thus enlisted them also for precisely opposite reasons.

From the beginning the rebels made great play with allegations of atrocities on the part of the police and other Security Forces. The booklet already quoted, which was issued in 1953 by the Naga Goodwill Mission to Assam, goes so far as to say that the Government of India 'had instructed their Indian Armed Forces to rape Naga women whenever and wherever possible.' It also accuses them of stealing food and drink from Naga houses, fruit and vegetables from their gardens and grain from their fields, and of robbing the forests of Naga timber as well as 'violating the sanctity of our religion and customs'. It further charges Government with 'detestable crimes' committed 'by their police forces and soldiers through encouragement given from the high authorities, torturing the helpless prisoners, beating and kicking them day and night, denying them sleep and refusing them to have clothes, putting them to starvation for days together'.

These allegations have been repeated year after year right up to the present day, but it is interesting that they have had less effect on the villagers than any of the other grievances which the NNC propagandists have emphasised. A Naga recently said to me that the people regarded the making of such accusations as un-Naga behaviour. 'We are warriors', he said, 'and we know that when we go to fight we are likely to get hurt. If we are, a true Naga will not whine about it.'

Another reason was that the people themselves realized that the great majority of these allegations had no basis in fact.

Finally, Naga fears for their land and culture were expressed by Mr Sakhrie:

'The tillers of the soil who had grown and lived on the land know the precious value of the land to which they are affectionately attached. Living their lives in their mystic mountain homes, the villagers had felt a threat to their old way of living, their freedom, their valued traditions, their customary laws, their land and their very existence. They wanted to preserve their race, their land, their freedom, and everything that was their's but began to wonder if, in the changing context of things, it would be possible any more.'

In this they were a little inconsistent, for the missionaries, through whom many of them were converted, interfered in their social and cultural practices far more than any Government could ever have done. They insisted on a convert becoming a teetotaller; he had to restrict himself to one wife : at one time he was not even allowed to eat the flesh of the mithun since this animal was associated with sacrifices at 'heathen' festivals. The missionaries stopped the great Feasts of Merit. They forbade boys to attend the Morungs (men's dormitories). They often stopped dancing, and even the art of weaving suffered since generally the convert adopted European mill-made dress. In the Sixth Schedule on the other hand, emphatic measures of protection of tribal culture and economic interests were included.

The causes of the Naga movement thus differ from those which have excited tribal people in other parts of India and of the world. There was, in fact, no colonising of the hills by outsiders; no one expropriated Naga land; there was little or no interference in tribal forest rights; there was little commercial exploitation and, except in regard to head-hunting, no official interference whatever in Naga culture or social custom.

But psychological anxiety and suspicion can be as tormenting as actual wrong, and can be as strong an incentive to revolt. In the case of the Nagas, the ideological factor was always dominant.

The Government of India's Reaction

What was the Government of India's reaction to all this ? It is important that we understand its attitude for, in spite of irresponsible statements by some politicians, it did consider the future of the Nagas with great sympathy and its decisions were not taken lightly. Why, it may be asked, did not the Government allow the Nagas to separate from India if they wanted to ? Would it have really mattered very much ?

I obviously cannot speak for the Indian Government, but I have studied the matter carefully and, so far as I can make out, its attitude was something like this. In the first place, it knew that the whole of the area now to be included under Nagaland was undisputed Indian territory and had always been recognized as such; the many different tribes living there were enjoying all the privileges of Indian citizenship and were already specially protected on the very points which had excited them to demand separation. The fact that in the composition of these tribes there were different elements was no more a justification for their separation from India than the multiracial elements which can be traced in almost all the different groups that compose the Indian population. Indeed countries throughout the world, and not least Great Britain and America, are inhabited by people of different racial stocks, whose blending has been a source of strength and variety.

Rabindranath Tagore, in his poem *Bharata-Tirtha*, speaks of 'the many streams of men which have flowed in resistless tides from places unknown and were lost in the one sea of India : here Aryan and non-Aryan, Dravidian, Chinese, the bands of the Sakas and Hunas, and Pathan and Moghul, have become combined in one body : the door to the West has also been opened, and they bring presents from there : they will give and they will take, they will unite and be united, and will never go away—in this ocean-shore of the Great Humanity of India.' This belief in the diverse origin and character of her culture is very deep in the Indian mind.

The Indian Government was also not convinced that the demand for complete separation from India was really supported by more than a minority, a strong minority it is true, of the entire population and that, where it was supported, it was for the wrong reasons. The people of Tuensang, until some of them were roused by a visit from Naga agitators in 1953, not only had no desire for separation but had welcomed the initiation of development activities. The great mass of the people who, in spite of occasional intervillage feuds, were in the main enjoying a happy life in their villages, tilling their fields, weaving their cloth, celebrating their festivals, attending their churches, had little inclination for leaving the protection of a country that offered them a settled Government, had brought head-hunting almost to an end and was rapidly introducing many of the amenities of modern life, for the dubious advantage of a theoretical independence which might deprive them of these benefits.

It was also inevitable—I am now looking at the problem from the angle of the whole country—that India should not be enthusiastic about the creation of a small independent sovereign State, which would always be badly in need of money, on one of her critical frontiers. The chances of such a State continuing to remain really independent for even as long as a decade appeared to her remote. The strongly Christian outlook of the Naga leaders has always kept them opposed to Communism, and some of them have now realised that India's argument had something in it.

There was no question whatever of India desiring to 'conquer' the Naga hills or to hold it for her own advantage. For what advantage was there ? The area was not one where colonists could find good jobs for their sons, for the policy has always been to administer it through its own people as they became educated. On the financial side, its retention cannot be regarded as a good bargain. The total income of the area is about £40,000 a year. Government's expenditure on administration and development is in the nature of three million pounds, or eighty times as much.

At the same time I think there can be no doubt that from the humanitarian point of view there were great advantages to the Nagas themselves in remaining within India's boundaries. To go outside would, almost inevitably, bring them under a far heavier control than was involved in their equal participation in the governance of a democratic India and there was no certainty as to their fate. India with her great plans for development, spread over periods of five years at a time, was confident that she could help the Nagas to progress in every way without interference with their customs and along the lines of their own genius. She had already made provision to protect Naga rights in land and forests, to give every Naga complete freedom to practise his own religion or to change it if he so desired, and to enjoy all the privileges of citizenship. She had given assurances that there would be no interference in the Nagas' customary law, their culture, their habits of food and drink and no introduction of alien taboos. Among a people

PHOTO: S. SEN

NAGA GIRLS ON THEIR WAY TO SCHOOL

Mr. Nehru meets Naga dancers attending a folk-dance festival at New Delhi

who had so recently abandoned head-hunting and where there were still inter-tribal and inter-village rivalries and feuds, India felt that the maintenance of law and order, which only she could ensure, was vital for the happiness of the common man.

This kind of argument has always, of course, been common among Imperialists anxious to justify their rule over weaker nations. But this is not so here, for the Nagas are not foreigners but are members of the one Indian family. A mother caring for her own children is something quite different from a wicked uncle exploiting someone else's children for his own advantage.

But why then did not India offer the Nagas a separate State within the Union at least six years ago when agitation was at its height ?

In the first place, the politically-minded Nagas did not ask for it. At that time, they only wanted a State outside the Indian Union. Even if it had been offered, few of the local leaders would have accepted it, for the extremists who were then very strong, wanted something quite different. Under the Sixth Schedule, which I have already described, India had offered the Nagas a large measure of self-government. It was not all that the Nagas wanted but it was a good deal and pamphlets were in fact distributed saying that if its provisions were found inadequate it could be considered for revision later.

The rejection by the Nagas of this admittedly preliminary, but educational, scheme to fit them for fuller responsibilities did not encourage the Government of India to make a more elaborate arrangement for them until they had at least tried it.

Another point that undoubtedly influenced Government was the reflection that it had only very recently achieved the consolidation of the country as a whole. The integration of the territories formerly ruled by the Indian princes into a united democratic body was a tremendous achievement. The unity of the great population of India with all its variety of race, religion, custom and language is a unique feature of its life. At the same time there were signs that this unity had to be carefully guarded. Linguistic minorities were clamouring for special treatment. There were even attempts to create small geographical units on a semi-religious basis. Some of the hill people of Assam were demanding a separate State for themselves. Government felt that anything that would endanger the remarkable unity in diversity that had been achieved should be resisted.

Government also felt that to create States with very small populations (Nagaland has a population of only 3,50,000 individuals which approximates to that of an average Sub-Division in Uttar Pradesh, and is only 6,236 square miles in extent, the size of an average District, of which there are several hundreds in the country) which were not viable and showed little hope of being viable for a very long time, was financially and administratively unsound.

It became, however, in the end a matter of balancing advantages—or disadvantages. Government, supported unanimously by public opinion throughout the country, regarded the creation of a sovereign Naga State outside India as unrealistic, and unsupported by law, history or commonsense; it felt that even a separate Nagaland within India might not be in the best interests of the Nagas and that certainly so long as a violent revolution was in progress there was no point in attempting a political settlement. But by the middle of 1960, although a hard core of rebel resistance still continued, the situation had greatly improved and at last there was a representative body of Nagas with whom it was possible to deal. It was now clear that nothing less than Nagaland—within India but with a large measure of autonomy—would satisfy the Nagas, and India's strongly democratic spirit prompted her to agree to its creation.

VI

SIXTEENTH STATE

The Naga delegation which went to New Delhi in July 1960 consisted of fifteen members and four consultants representing all the main Naga tribes. They presented the 16-point Memorandum on which the Mokokchung Convention had agreed and discussed it thoroughly with senior officials of the Ministry of External Affairs, finally presenting to the Prime Minister a version which was slightly modified to suit the provisions of the Constitution. During the discussions everyone seems to have got on very well with each other and the approach to the problem was marked by commonsense and realism.

The final decision was announced by the Prime Minister in Parliament on 1st August 1960. Briefly stated, it agreed that a new State to be called 'Nagaland' would be established within the Indian Union comprising the territory of the existing Naga Hills Tuensang Area (NHTA). The same person would be appointed as the Governor of Assam and the Governor of Nagaland and the existing jurisdiction of the Assam High Court would continue. There would be a transitional period during which an interim body would be constituted with representatives from every Naga tribe to assist and advise the Governor in the administration of Nagaland. The Governor would have special responsibility for law and order during this transitional period or for so long as disturbances continued. Since the financial resources of the new State would be extremely limited, and large grants from the Central Government might be necessary, not only for development schemes, but also to maintain the efficiency of the administration, the Governor would have general responsibility for ensuring that the funds made available by the Government of India were expended for the purpose for which they were approved.

There would be a Legislative Assembly to which the Council of Ministers of the new State would be responsible. Certain safeguards, similar to those in the existing Sixth Schedule of the Constitution, would be provided for the religious and social practices of the Nagas, Naga customary laws and procedure and the ownership and transfer of land. Otherwise, the existing laws relating to the administration of civil and criminal justice would continue to remain in force. Special provision would be made for the administration of the Tuensang District in accordance with the wishes of its people.

This was the main decision, but the details of the agreement, though not of much interest to the general reader (who can skip the rest of this Chapter), are of importance to those who have been following developments among the Nagas during the last few years.

Ao girl (*after* Mills, 1926)

Let us, therefore, now examine the Memorandum, as it was finally revised, point by point.

The first Section, of fundamental importance, runs as follows:—

'The territories that were heretofore known as the Naga Hills Tuensang Area under the Naga Hills-Tuensang Area Act, 1957 shall form a State within the Indian Union and be hereafter known as Nagaland.'

The name of the new State has been criticised, yet if its derivation from the word *nok* or 'people' is correct, Nagaland has the attractive meaning of 'Land of People' who will look on themselves and others simply as human beings, free of racial, communal and caste distinctions and antagonisms.

The Nagas desired that the new State should be under the Ministry of External Affairs, for they felt that they had been with this Ministry previously and would feel more at home in dealing with it than with the Government of India as a whole. This provision, however, cannot be written into the Constitution.

The third point laid down that the President of India should appoint a Governor for Nagaland with his headquarters within the State. The original suggestion had been that there should be a separate Governor but after considerable argument the Nagas accepted the fact that this would be a heavy strain on their finances and finally agreed that the same person should be appointed both as Governor of Assam and as Governor of Nagaland in view of the fact that the Constitution provides for the appointment of the same person as Governor of two or more States. This will, in fact, mean that the Governor will have one headquarters in Shillong and another in Nagaland and will divide his time between them.

It was obvious that it would be wise, in view of the limited resources of the new State, to avoid an elaborate administrative apparatus, but no objection was raised to the formation of a regular Secretariat headed by a Chief Secretary. An important provision lays down that 'the Governor shall have special responsibility with regard to law and order during the transitional period and for so long as the law and order situation continues to remain disturbed on account of hostile activities. In exercising this special responsibility, the Governor shall, after consultation with the Ministry, act in his individual judgement. This special responsibility of the Governor will cease when normalcy returns.'

Section 4 provides for a Council of Ministers with a Chief Minister, which will be responsible to the Naga Legislative Assembly. This Assembly will consist of elected and nominated members as may be considered necessary to represent different tribes. Although the delegation had originally asked for three elected members to represent Nagaland in the Union Parliament, they finally agreed to two, one for the Lok Sabha and the other for the Rajya Sabha, in view of the fact that in other States representation is linked to population.

Section 7 gives protection to Naga law and customs and runs as follows—

'No Act or Law passed by the Union Parliament affecting the following provisions shall have legal force in Nagaland unless specifically applied to it by a majority vote of the Naga Legislative Assembly—

1) Religious or social practices.
2) Customary Naga laws and procedure.
3) Civil and Criminal Justice so far as these concern decisions according to Naga Customary Law. The existing laws relating to administration of civil and criminal justice as provided in the Rules for the administration of Justice and Police in the Naga Hills District shall continue to be in force.
4) The ownership and transfer of land and its resources.'

The traditional system of tribal councils is continued in Section 8:

'Each tribe shall have the following units of rule-making and administrative local bodies to deal with matters concerning the respective tribes and areas :—

1) The Village Council
2) The Range Council
3) The Tribal Council.

'These Councils will also deal with disputes and cases involving breaches of customary laws and usages.

'Appeals will lie to (1) the District Court-cum-Sessions Court (for each District), the High Court of Assam and the Supreme Court o India and (2) the Naga Tribunal (for the whole of the Nagaland) in respect of cases decided according to Customary Law.'

In view of the fact that the Tuensang District came under regular administration much later than the Naga Hills District, the inhabitants themselves had insisted and the Naga delegation as a whole had agreed that special provisions should be made for it. It was decided that the Governor shall carry on its administration for ten years until the Tuensang tribes are capable of shouldering the 'heavier responsibilities of an advanced system of administration'. It will have a Regional Council consisting of elected representatives of all the tribes in the District, to which the Governor may also nominate members; the Deputy Commissioner will be its ex-officio Chairman; and it will elect representatives from among its members to the Naga Legislative Assembly. It is provided that no Act or Law passed by the main Assembly shall be applicable to Tuensang unless it is specifically recommended by the Regional Council. At the end of ten years the situation will be reviewed and, if the people so desire, the period of special treatment will be extended.

A very serious problem facing the new State is Finance. The revenues of Nagaland will be very limited and it will have to depend on grants from the Central Government both for development and perhaps for some time for the cost of administration. All States are subject to some measure of control by the Government of India in respect of the amounts which they receive from it and Nagaland, like other States, will have to follow the usual procedures. Section 11, therefore, runs as follows—

'To supplement the revenues of Nagaland, there will be need for the Government of India to pay out of the Consolidated Fund of India

1) a lump sum each year for the development programme in Nagaland, and

2) a grant-in-aid towards meeting the cost of administration.

'Proposals for these grants will be prepared and submitted by the Government of Nagaland to the Government of India for its approval. The Governor will have general responsibility for ensuring that these funds are expended for the purpose for which they have been approved.'

Naga in ceremonial dress

Section 12 refers to certain Reserved Forests which had formed part of the Naga Hills District from 1882 to 1903, but which, since 1903, have been part of the Sibsagar and Nowgong Districts of Assam. It was not possible to make any decision at the time but the delegation expressed its desire that the following should be placed on record:—

'The Naga delegation discussed the question of the inclusion of the Reserved Forests and of contiguous areas inhabited by the Nagas. They were referred to the provisions in Articles 3 and 4 of the Constitution, prescribing the procedure for the transfer of areas from one State to another.'

In the same way, the delegation had urged that Nagas living within other areas could join the new State if they so desired. In view of the fact, however, that the territory of Nagaland would have to be stated precisely in the First Schedule of the Constitution, if it was to come into being as a State, Government could not accept this but the delegation wished that the following should be placed on record under Section 13:—

'The Naga leaders expressed the view that other Nagas inhabiting contiguous areas should be enabled to join the new State. It was pointed out to them on behalf of the Government of India that Articles 3 and 4 of the Constitution provided for increasing the area of any State, but that it was not possible for the Government of India to make any commitment in this regard at this stage.'

In Section 14 of their Memorandum the delegation had urged that in order that the Naga people could fulfil their desire to play a full role in the defence forces of India, a separate Naga Regiment should be raised. There are, of course, already companies of Nagas in the existing Battalions of the Assam Regiment and this suggestion was accepted for examination.

It was not intended by the delegation that all the provisions contained in the agreement should be implemented immediately and Section 15, therefore, reads thus:—

'(*a*) On reaching a political settlement with the Government of India, the Government of India will prepare a Bill for such amendment of the Constitution, as may be necessary, in order to implement the decisions and the Draft Bill, before presentation to Parliament, will be shown to the delegates of the NPC.

'(*b*) There shall be constituted an Interim Body with elected representatives from every tribe, to assist and advise the Governor in the administration of Nagaland during the transitional period. The tenure of office of the Interim Body will be three years subject to re-election.'

Finally, Section 16 refers to the Inner Line Regulation, already discussed in Chapter II, and lays down hat rules embodied in the Bengal Eastern Frontier Regulation, 1873, shall remain in force in Nagaland. That the Nagas themselves should desire the continuation of this regulation, which has been so strongly criticized by non-tribals, is surely significant.

On the 1st of August, 1960 the Prime Minister announced the terms of the agreement in the Lok Sabha and said that his Government would shortly introduce a Bill to constitute Nagaland the sixteenth State in India. He concluded his speech by saying that 'We have always regarded the territory inhabited by the Nagas as part of independent India as defined in our Constitution. We looked upon all these tribal people as citizens of independent India having all the privileges and obligations of such citizenship.

'The Nagas are a hard-working and disciplined people, and there is much in their way of life from which others can learn with profit. We have had for many years Nagas in the Indian Army and they have proved to be excellent soldiers. Our policy has always been to give the fullest autonomy and opportunity of self-Government to the Naga people without interfering in any way in their internal affairs or way of life.'

The reaction throughout India was generally favourable. A couple of small reactionary and communal political parties declared their opposition; a few newspapers voiced their fears about possible consequences elsewhere. But Members of Parliament, the bulk of the Press, and the people even in Assam greeted the settlement and gave a warm welcome to the young State that is to be.

The Home Minister, Pandit G. B. Pant expressed the feeling of the whole country when he said: 'We have been living together for ages and it is a matter of pride to all of us that we belong to this great country. We in India are not individuals; everyone has a backing of forty crores of people.

'The prizes of peace are more rewarding and abiding than those of friction.'

VII

ADVENTURES IN FRIENDSHIP

The great plans for the development of the hill and forest people, on which the Government of India is now spending very large sums of money, are essentially adventures in friendship. But though the Community Development programme, the development of agriculture and animal husbandry, the opening of schools, building of hospitals, making of roads, schemes for irrigation and so on are tokens—and expensive tokens—of that friendship, some of the most important matters do not cost anything at all. Perhaps the most important of these imponderables is the need to integrate, emotionally and psychologically, these long isolated people with the rest of India. Indeed, the idea of integration runs as a sort of theme song through all these plans.

This is a thing which cannot be bought with money. Unless development schemes are carried out in the right way they will not create a sense of friendliness and unity. The vital thing is that the tribal people should feel at home, with a full realisation that India is their country, the Government is their Government, that they belong to it and it belongs to them.

There is a great deal of money available for the development of the tribal areas, all of which will be covered with Community Development Blocks by 1963. At least one quarter of this should be used for developing communications in order to bring even the most distant villages out of their long isolation. A solution of this problem will mean increased material prosperity, the extension of the healing hand of modern medicine, the spread of new ideas. But we must bear in mind that this will not happen automatically. Accessibility can open the door to an enrichment of life, to a new understanding and friendliness, but it can also give opportunity for exploitation. This is why it is essential that general development should go hand in hand with the development of communications and this, in fact, is what is now planned.

Then an all-round system of education is necessary. We must cease to think of education as being confined to schools. Education in agriculture and animal husbandry is perhaps the most important of all, for the greatest tribal problem is poverty and hunger. There must be education too in the right use of forests and the right care of land.

I have already quoted Dr Radhakrishnan as saying that we must give up the 'big brother complex' in dealing with the tribes and 'approach them with affection and friendship and not condescension or contempt. Progress should be judged not merely by advances in technology but by the state of the human beings concerned and their relations with one another, The tribes should be made by our own behaviour to feel that they are an important and integral section of the Indian people.' This means that a great deal will depend on the attitude of officials, social workers, and indeed, of everyone who has to deal with the tribal people. Any attitude of scorn or patronage will undermine the very foundations of integration. This is why I so dislike the use of words like 'backward' and 'uplift', which imply that we are much better than these simple folk who, in fact, are ahead of us in many fundamental ways.

As the tribes are beginning to know more about their country and the equalitarian ideals that inspire it, they are becoming more and more sensitive to the importance of their own religion, their language and their culture generally. They are not likely to be attracted to India as a whole by workers who interfere with their customs, tell them that their ideas are all wrong and attempt to uproot them and force them to leave their loved hills and settle under artificial conditions at a distance from their ancestral lands. The creation of an inferiority complex is no basis for true friendship. We must not make the tribes ashamed of their own way of doing things and of their culture. On the contrary, there is so much good in what they have that there is every reason to develop and encourage it.

And this leads me to a very important point. In the old days all the stress was on what we should do for the tribal people. Today we are beginning to see that it is equally important to stress what the tribal people can do for us. It was Sir Akbar Hydari and his Chief Minister, Lokopriya Gopinath Bardoloi, who took the lead in developing this idea, which Mr N. K. Rustomji has defined as 'the concept of the people of the hills and plains living in equal partnership with each other, each pulsating in the country's being as one living body.' Once the tribes feel that they have something of their own which they can contribute to the infinite variety of India, that they are not just poor relations to be patronized, that they are really looked on as fellow human beings, exactly the same as everybody else, then the task of integration will be easier.

Education must be adapted so that it develops and does not destroy tribal culture and language. The economic status of the people must be greatly improved, for poverty is no basis for national enthusiasm. Roads must be built with sufficient safeguards so that their country is opened up not for exploitation but for their own benefit. They should be helped to visit other parts of India so that they can obtain a vision of what their country is.

We—the people of the towns and cities—must recognise and honour the tribals' way of doing things, not because it is old or picturesque but because it is their's, and they have as much right to their own culture and religion as anyone else in India. We must talk their language, and not only the language that is expressed in words but the deeper language of the heart. We must, in fact, 'think tribal'. We will not make the tribes ashamed of their past or force a sudden break with it, but we will help them to build upon it and grow by a natural process of evolution. This does not mean a policy of mere preservation; it implies a constant development and change, a change that in time will bring unbelievable enrichment, as there is ever closer integration in the main stream of Indian life, which has always been hospitable to a great variety of cultures.

Against this 'philosophical' background, development has, especially since Independence, been continuing fruitfully among the Nagas. There is a wonderful opportunity for it here, for the Nagas are live, vigorous, progressive and have a passion to bring their own area into line with the rest of India and the world.

Plans for Development

The development of the Naga Hills District had been making steady, though rather slow, progress in the latter years of the British period and at Independence there were, for example, 12 hospitals and a total of nearly 200 schools, of which 61 were private. There were, however, only 214 miles of motorable road in the entire District. When I visited Mokokchung in 1947 I had to make a journey of four days on foot to get there. Today the same journey can be made in a little over four hours.

After Independence and during the First Five Year Plan until disturbances began, development schemes started very hopefully, especially in Tuensang, to which any such idea was completely new. These plans all over India have aimed at raising the standard of living of the people by the improvement of communications, better agriculture and the provision of health and educational facilities, During the First Five Year Plan nearly a thousand miles of roads were constructed in the Naga Hills District and the number of schools more than doubled. The number of hospitals and dispensaries also considerably increased. Two National Extension Service Blocks were established in 1953-54 and three more were added later; between them they covered about half the entire area of the District.

Unhappily, after the outbreak of hostilities the programme for the early years of the Second Five Year Plan became almost completely ineffective for two or three years. Many people were hiding in the forest, and villages which co-operated in official schemes were attacked by the rebels. It was really only after the first Naga People's Convention held in August 1957 that the villagers recovered sufficient confidence to co-operate with Government in its plans, though even then they sometimes had to suffer intimidation and assault.

A Three-Year Plan

Since it was not possible to fulfil the programmes of the Second Five-Year Plan, a special Three-Year-Plan was inaugurated from 1958 onwards. This covers all the subjects included in the plans for other parts of India but is specially adapted to the conditions of Nagaland. The highest item of expenditure is on roads, which amounts to over 185 lakhs of rupees (nearly £ 1,400,000). Next comes Public Health and Water-Supply which comes to over 62 lakhs or £ 460,000, and Education which comes to nearly 47 lakhs (£ 350,000). Thirty-five lakhs or £ 260,000 goes for Community Development; and Agriculture and Animal Husbandry account for over 16 lakhs (£ 120,000) out of a total of approximately 380 lakhs of rupees (£ 2,840,000) spread over a period of three years.

Education

For the Nagas perhaps the most important aspect of progress is in the field of education, for which there is a great demand. As we have seen, the first Naga school was opened by a missionary, the Rev. Miles Bronson, as far back as the forties of the last century, and in the intervening period there has been steady progress in the opening of schools, some of them missionary schools, as a result of which many Nagas have qualified as officials, teachers and technicians. During the disturbances of 1955-56, however, education came almost to a standstill. The rebels insisted that schools should be closed and school-masters were asked to stop teaching. Many schools were burnt, in Tuensang District alone fifteen being destroyed by the rebels, though a few struggled on.

After the inception of the NHTA administration in December 1957, however, many schools were reopened and others were started. Today there are 7 High Schools, 49 Middle Schools, 411 Lower Primary Schools, a Basic Training Centre for teachers and a technical institution, catering for about 47,000 students in all. There has been an increasing provision of Hindi teachers to meet the growing demand from Nagas anxious to learn the national language. In the Kohima District, for example, seventeen of the eighteen M. E. Schools have

Mokokchung High School

Hindi teachers on their staff. The Mokokchung High School, which like the Kohima school is built on a beautiful site with distant views, has 330 girls among its 1,119 students. So strong is the desire for education that in many villages the people have opened schools at their own expense and the Rengma and Chakhesang Nagas have even started High Schools for themselves. In Mokokchung the people have collected money to start a college which they named after the late Mr S. Fazl Ali, a former Governor of Assam. For higher education 157 stipends and scholarships to the value of about £ 10,000 have been given in the last two years to the most promising Naga boys and girls.

Health Services

In 1957 there were 12 hospitals, 18 dispensaries and 5 mobile medical units in NHTA but during the disturbances most of these, except the hospitals at Headquarters, were closed down as a result of looting by the rebels and in some cases the abduction of the medical staff. During the last three years, however, great progress has been made. Today there are 24 hospitals, 23 dispensaries and no fewer than 66 doctors, 83 compounders and 23 nurses. Anyone who knows the extreme difficulty of obtaining medical staff willing to go into the tribal areas in other parts of India will realize the great achievement of the NHTA Administration in having attracted so many workers at a time of crisis.

The new hospital at Mokokchung will be a splendid affair when it is ready, and a whole section of the town has been set apart for medical services. One feature of the medical work here is its mobility and a temporary twenty-bedded hospital can be set up anywhere in the District that is accessible by road within forty-eight hours.

It is obviously impossible to open a dispensary in every village, but with the great increase in roads, mobile health units have assumed a new importance. Specially adapted jeep ambulances are now moving about the country for the treatment of villagers in their own homes and to bring serious cases into hospital.

Malaria is one of the chief health problems of Nagaland and an anti-malaria unit with eight centres and nearly 250 field workers trained in anti-malaria duties has been started. The spraying of DDT, and the distribution of preventive medicines is continuing. Another rather common disease among the Nagas is Hansen's Disease. In 1959, a 50-bed colony for sufferers from this was started at Longleng in the Tuensang District and is now being expanded to take 100 patients. A second colony for 100 patients is being started this year at Tansangti in the Kohima District.

Tuberculosis is less common among the Nagas than it is, for example, among the people of Siang, but BCG vaccination was begun, for the first time in the Naga hills, in March 1959 and over 60,000 people have so far been treated. A 50-bed T. B. hospital in Mokokchung is nearly ready, on which about 6 lakhs of rupees (£ 45,000) have been spent.

A Good Water-Supply

Nearly all Naga villages are perched on the tops of hills for security reasons. In the old days they were often surrounded by palisades and walls and there were look-out places and guard-houses from which the people could obtain wide views of the surrounding area and could see any enemies coming to attack them. The position of these villages has meant that most Nagas live under conditions of enchanting beauty. At the same time it has also meant that they suffer from lack of water, which girls may have to climb down a steep hill for a thousand feet or more to draw in their great bamboo tubes, while the use of local pits and ponds has led to a wide incidence of intestinal diseases. The provision of a good water-supply for every village is a scheme that is beyond controversy and already some 135 villages have been equipped with wells or pipes and there are plans that within the next two or three years every single village will have a good protected water-supply.

Communications

The improvement of communications is of major importance for the progress of the isolated tribal areas throughout India. Roads extend the possibility of trade. They bring medical and other facilities to the very doors of the people and promote the spread of new ideas. Road-building in the Naga Hills goes back to the seventies of the last century but during the last two years there has been an unprecedented advance. 140 miles of new roads have been made, another 330 miles have been widened and improved and 6 major bridges have been built in Kohima District alone. In Mokokchung the record is even better, for there have been 185 miles of new roads and the improvement of another 490 with 15 new bridges. In the Tuensang District, however, which is more remote, where labour is scarce and where the gradients are very steep, there has been less progress but even so, 25 miles of road have been built, 180 miles improved and 24 new bridges have been made as well as 375 miles of mule-paths and bridle tracks. The National Highway from Dimapur leading to Imphal through Kohima has been improved at the cost of 10 lakhs of rupees (£ 75,000).

Electric Power

To those who knew the Naga area twenty or even ten years ago, it will be strange to read of the introduction of electric power. The Nagas themselves started two small hydro-electric schemes shortly after the last World War and now Government has taken up the electrification of seven small towns. Kohima town and the neighbouring villages have been supplied with light and power and in Dimapur the scheme will shortly be completed.

PHOTO: LIBERTY NEWS PICTURES, DELHI

THE NAGA DELEGATION OF 1960 CARRIES A WREATH TO MAHATMA GANDHI'S MEMORIAL IN NEW DELHI

Agriculture

The Naga method of raising food-crops has always been by shifting cultivation, although the Angamis and some other tribes who have come under their influence have excellent terraces, and potato crops were introduced many years ago. Shifting cultivation is laborious and, although not so destructive of the forest or so liable to cause erosion as was at one time believed, is obviously an undesirable and wasteful method. The Administration, therefore, has, for some

Terracing in the Angami hills

time past, tried to teach the people new methods of permanent cultivation and in the last two years nearly 5,000 acres of virgin land have been reclaimed. 4,000 acres are under wet rice cultivation, for which over 300 irrigation channels have been constructed and an extensive scheme of agricultural education has been started. The application of modern science to shifting cultivation has great possibilities and this is necessary because there are many areas in these formidable hills where there is no alternative land available. Large numbers of tools and implements, new kinds of seed, fertilizers and indeed, the entire apparatus of agricultural improvement which is being introduced all over India is coming also to the Naga area, and in the last two years it is claimed that there has been over 30 per cent increase in the production of food. Horticulture is not neglected and new cash crops and vegetable gardens are being introduced.

Some of the new development projects have been undertaken in memory of courageous Nagas who suffered at the hands of their own people. A hostel for 100 boys attached to the Kohima High School has been erected and named after Mr Sakhrie. A permanent bridge on the Kohima-Chakhabama road has been named after the late Subedar Satsuo Angami. He was the first Naga to be returned to the Assam Legislative Assembly and the first Angami to become a Viceroy's Commissioned Officer in the Army. Formerly an important member of the NNC, he later resigned and raised Village Guards in Kohima District. He was murdered by the rebels, shot in the back through a window of his house, as he was addressing a meeting.

Community Development

There are at present nine Community Development Blocks covering an area of 4,217 square miles and a population of a little over 2,00,000 people. The programme, which is realistic and confined to basic needs has been specially adapted to local and tribal conditions with special stress on communications, agriculture, animal husbandry and irrigation.

Arts and Crafts

The Nagas are a hard-working and artistic people and they have many traditional cottage industries. The problem here is not to teach industries so much as to increase production and supply the villagers with raw materials. In the Tuensang District, however, there are two Cottage Industries Training and Production Centres in which carpentry, blacksmithy, masonry are being taught and wood-carving is being encouraged. Here and in Mokokchung District there are emporia in which the finest local products are kept on show and will form the nucleus of peoples' museums which will be started in the near future.

They also stock local products for sale. There is a similar emporium in Kohima and a Junior Technical School, which was started many years ago, will shortly be converted into a polytechnical institute. When this is started it will train boys in carpentry, blacksmithy, masonry, tailoring, paper-making and, it is hoped, will ultimately turn out electricians, draftsmen and overseers.

Lhota Naga design

Women's Centres

A maternity and child-welfare centre was opened at Kohima at the beginning of 1959 and is now serving as an inspiration for similar institutions elsewhere. The centre trains midwives for other areas and gives an opportunity to Naga women, who have been made destitute by rebel activity, to earn their living. There are a score of such women working as weavers here and others do their weaving at home and bring their textiles in for sale : others are learning to knit.

Nagas for Nagaland

A very important aspect of development here is that already much of it is being done by the Nagas themselves. The number employed even before the agreement on Nagaland is striking. In the General Administration Department there were two Nagas against six outsiders in the highest grade, but there were 32 against 17 in Class II, 385 against 180 in Class III and 230 against 29 in Class IV, a total of 649 Nagas as compared with 232 non-Naga officials in this important branch of the Administration.

In the Medical Department, there were only 8 Naga doctors against 55 non-Nagas, but there were 336 Naga nurses, compounders and attendants compared to 88 others. Similarly in the Agriculture and Veterinary Department, both the higher officers were Nagas, and there were 340 Nagas in the other grades and only 21 others. It is true that all the seven Class I engineers were non-Naga and there were only 52 Naga Class II and technical employees in Class III combined against 90 others in the Engineering branch. But had Naga engineers been available, they would have been engaged immediately. The highest proportion of Naga employees was in the Education Department where there were 988 Nagas and only 87 others.

Total employment comes to 2,515 Nagas and 809 outsiders. That the majority of the technical staff, especially in the fields of Health and Engineering, should be drawn from outside is only natural; as the Nagas themselves take up these professions the position will soon be reversed.

The Third Five-Year Plan

Under the programme for the Third Five-Year Plan, all these schemes will be extended until the whole of Nagaland, to the most distant ranges of its hills, is covered, and the work on existing schemes will be intensified.

Ao Naga textile design

VIII

THE FUTURE OF NAGALAND

ANYTHING is possible to the Naga people. Secure in their own villages and towns, their land guaranteed, their forests protected, with ample funds available from the Government of India which treasures their co-operation, with the splendid resources of their own energy, imagination and intelligence, there is no reason why, if they can preserve their unity, they should not build up a really progressive State. The highest positions in the country are open to everyone, irrespective of caste, creed or community: there is nothing to prevent a Naga becoming President or Prime Minister or holding one of the coveted posts that reward effective service of the country.

Material progress is within the Nagas' grasp. New methods of agriculture with animal husbandry, improved seed, extended irrigation, fertilizers to make their already fertile hills more productive, and new implements will help them to have more, much more food. A great net-work of roads and bridges will help to create unity among those who have been divided from one another by towering hills and raging torrents. Until the Nagas can produce their own, devoted doctors from other parts of India will come to work with them as friends: there are already many Naga girls who have become nurses. Electricity will bring power and light and solve many practical problems. The Nagas will explore and exploit their mineral and forest wealth, and as they develop their arts, these will, if they are in line with their own traditions, find a ready market and bring more money to them.

The spread of education, if we are to judge by what has already happened, will be rapid; if it has a sufficiently technical bias, before long Nagas themselves will not only be laying down policies in their Legislature but will be themselves implementing them as engineers, doctors, teachers and agriculturalists in the field.

I have little doubt that with the growth of material prosperity there will be a cultural and spiritual renaissance. Naga dancing is famous and as the people dance more thay will revive in their hearts old memories and joys. The Nagas have excellent taste, a perfect sense of colour, and there are welcome signs that they will not permit a so-called modernism to banish colour from their lives and depress them into the drab uniformity of the dress and ornamentation of today. Naga music and singing can be beautiful and need not be destroyed, as traditional music has been destroyed in so many parts of the world, by a slavish imitation of the cinema hit or rock 'n roll.

Many of the Nagas are Christians: I hope the form of Christianity they follow will broaden out and adjust itself to the modern world. Many others follow their own traditional faith. But whatever religion they observe, it is essential that the spiritual values of life are not forgotten in the excitement of material advance. Specially important are the great virtues of compassion and forgiveness. I was struck, as were many others, by the friendliness of the members of the Naga delegation who came to Delhi in July 1960. I found the same attitude during a recent tour in all the Naga Districts. There was no bitterness, no harping on wrongs. This spirit of mutual forgiveness must also spread among the Nagas themselves. The blood-feud is deep in Naga psychology, and in the last few years the rebels have sown many seeds of vengeance which must be uprooted if Nagaland is to progress. The rebels are fellow citizens, fellow human beings, and any desire for revenge will be a sterilizing and frustrating force.

Perhaps the greatest achievement of the Naga awakening has been to unite the formerly divided and warring tribes into what is now largely a single body with one aim, the welfare and progress of the new State that is to be. As political and judicial institutions develop, tribesmen whose loyalty for centuries has been restricted to their own village or their own tribe will feel more and more their responsibility for the whole body of their fellows. As Naga representatives in Parliament and the Rajya Sabha take more part in the general affairs of the nation, as the Nagas come to know the rest of India better, this sense of responsibility will grow more widely, until at last they will take their part in the One World of our dreams.

For the Nagas have a great contribution to make to India. On the practical side they have given many loyal and efficient officials to the services; there are nine Naga officers in the Indian Frontier Administrative Service, one of whom has been awarded the Padma Shri; others hold important posts in the Assam State. Naga soldiers of various ranks are playing a valuable part in the Indian Army and we have already noted the Naga share in two World Wars: in the second, three Nagas received the M.C., nine the M.M., one the I.D.M.S.: and six Naga civilians the M.B.E. In the field of athletics, Nagas are taking a leading part in many schools and colleges and in the Defence Services. An Ao Naga captained the Indian Football team at the Olympic Games in London in 1948 and on its Far East tour in 1951.

It will be for the future to decide what influence the Kirata or Indo-Mongoloid population, in which the Nagas are included, will have on the mentality and culture of India as a whole, and it has been suggested that it will be a 'temperamental' rather than a material or spiritual contribution. This is an interesting idea and, though today there are signs that the Indo-Mongoloids may give a new and tonic inspiration to the textile and other arts, it is probably true that their most substantial contribution will be in the field of character and temperament.

It will be worth while, therefore, to glance at some of the psychological imponderables that distinguish the Nagas. The first is the exceptionally co-operative character of the village community, which works as a whole for agriculture, ceremonial and, today, for 'development'. In the past, there has been a tendency for the villages to turn inwards on themselves, ignoring the interests of their neighbours, and today there is some danger of a new religious individualism weakening the corporate spirit, yet on the whole progress is in the direction of a wider vision, which to some extent is counteracting the separateness caused by the great distances and the memories of war and feud.

Then the Nagas are very self-reliant. The country is so hard and the conditions of life in the past have been so severe that only the strongest have survived. Even though until recently they have had little medical assistance and are still often short of food, many of them are splendid specimens of humanity. In the past they did everything for themselves, constructed their inter-village paths, built their bridges and gave relief to one another in time of need. They have made their own cloth, their own hats and rain-coats; they have prepared their own medicines, their own cooking-vessels, their own substitutes for crockery; some of them even have their own cosmetics. They have made and administered their own laws.

Although for hundreds of years the Nagas resented the visits of strangers, their former attitude was probably due to a rather natural suspicion and fear; today they are the most open-hearted and generous of people, and the spirit of hospitality, which was always one of the most treasured of virtues as among themselves, is now extended to their visitors. The traditional Naga attitude to property is a rather charming one. The honourable thing was to get rid of it. The Feasts of Merit, which bestowed so much distinction on their donors, showed that it was the distribution of wealth rather than its possession that was important. And this distribution included everyone, not merely one's own relations and rich friends, but the poorest and least important.

Although there is no matriarchy among the Nagas, women hold a high and honourable position. They work on equal terms with the men in the fields and make their influence felt in the tribal councils. The wives of the great Konyak nobles are very fine ladies, possessed of a natural grace and dignity; they have many privileges and social duties. The educated are among the most graceful and charming of India's womanhood.

A belief in the importance of loyalty, a hardness of moral and physical fibre, courage before impossible living conditions, the love of adventure and exploration, a fresh, candid, simple attitude to life's problems are among the other qualities that the Nagas, along with many other hill people, have to give the world.

As mankind moves forward to the fulfilment of its destiny, it will fail unless it can banish fear and suspicion, hatred and the spirit of revenge; separateness and xenophobia are today spiritually out of date; to be 'modern' is to love and to unite. If Nagaland can realise that Angami and Sema, Konyak and Ao, rebel and liberal, hillman and plainsman are 'but alternate beats of the same heart', it will have a great and happy future. The story of India has been, in Dr S. K. Chatterji's words, 'a synthesis of races and cultures leading to the creation and characterization of a composite Indian people and a composite Indian civilization, diverse in its origin but united in its ideals and aspirations—ideals and aspirations which are acceptable to all mankind; while India looks forward to a still greater unification of all mankind, both within her shores and outside.'

As Nagaland realises its position in the great country of which it is so precious a part, it will share in the fulfilment of this ideal.

NOTE

Surprisingly little has been written about the Nagas in recent years, and the standard works on the different tribes, admirable as they are, are now many years out of date and have long been out of print.

For the general background of culture and tradition, however, the following may still be consulted with profit and enjoyment:

J. H. Hutton, *The Angami Nagas* (London, 1921)
J. H. Hutton, *The Sema Nagas* (London, 1921)
J. P. Mills, *The Lhota Nagas* (London, 1922)
J. P. Mills, *The Ao Nagas* (London, 1926)
C. von Furer-Haimendorf, *The Naked Nagas* (London, 1932)
J. P. Mills, *The Rengma Nagas* (London, 1937)

My debt to the above and particularly to Dr J. H. Hutton will be frequently apparent.

Other books of considerable value, on the historical side, are:

A. Mackenzie, *History of the Relations of Government with the Hill Tribes of the North-East Frontier of Bengal* (Calcutta, 1884)
R. Reid, *History of the Frontier Areas bordering on Assam from 1883-1941* (Shillong, 1942)
L.W. Shakespear, *History of Upper Assam, Burmah and North-Eastern Frontier* (London, 1914)

On the Indo-Mongoloids, there is an important article by Dr Suniti Kumar Chatterji—'Kirata-Jana-Kriti: The Indo-Mongoloids: their Contribution to the History and Culture of India' in the *Journal of the Royal Asiatic Society of Bengal*, Vol. XVI, No. 2 (1950) on which I have drawn heavily.

Some material and many pictures illustrating the art of the Tuensang Nagas will be found in my own *The Art of the North-East Frontier of India* (Shillong, 1959)

I am grateful to Mr R. Bagchi who prepared the line-drawings, map and jacket and to all others, too numerous to mention by name, who helped me in the preparation of this book.

1.10.60

V.E.

INDEX

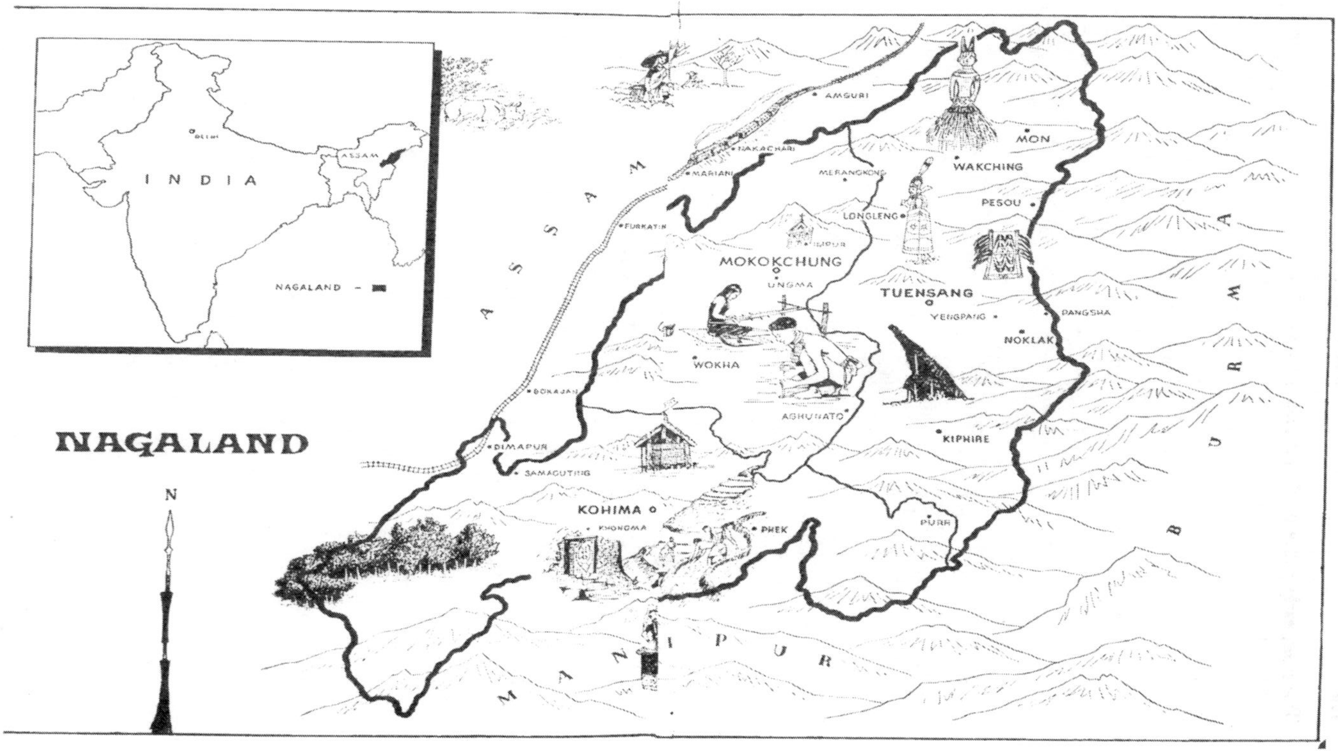
NAGALAND
N
INDIA
DELHI
ASSAM
NAGALAND —
ASSAM
BURMA
MANIPUR
MON
WAKCHING
PESOU
AMGURI
NAKACHARI
MARIANI
MERANGKONG
LONGLENG
FURKATIN
IMPUR
MOKOKCHUNG
UNGMA
TUENSANG
YENGPANG
DANGSHA
NOKLAK
WOKHA
BOKAJAN
AGHUNATO
KIPHIRE
DIMAPUR
SAMAGUTING
KOHIMA
KHONOMA
PHEK
PURR